The Upside of the Downturn

The Upside of the Downturn

Ten Management Strategies to Prevail
in the Recession and Thrive
in the Aftermath

GEOFF COLVIN

Portfolio

PORTFOLIO
Published by the Penguin Group
Penguin Group (USA) Inc.,
375 Hudson Street, New York, New York 10014, U.S.A.
Penguin Group (Canada), 90 Eglinton Avenue East,
Suite 700, Toronto, Ontario, Canada M4P 2Y3
(a division of Pearson Penguin Canada Inc.)
Penguin Books Ltd, 80 Strand, London WC2R 0RL, England
Penguin Ireland, 25 St. Stephen's Green, Dublin 2, Ireland
(a division of Penguin Books Ltd)
Penguin Books Australia Ltd, 250 Camberwell Road,
Camberwell, Victoria 3124, Australia
(a division of Pearson Australia Group Pty Ltd)
Penguin Books India Pvt Ltd, 11 Community Centre,
Panchsheel Park, New Delhi – 110 017, India
Penguin Group (NZ), 67 Apollo Drive, Rosedale, North Shore 0632,
New Zealand (a division of Pearson New Zealand Ltd)
Penguin Books (South Africa) (Pty) Ltd, 24 Sturdee Avenue,
Rosebank, Johannesburg 2196, South Africa

Penguin Books Ltd, Registered Offices:
80 Strand, London WC2R 0RL, England

First published in 2009 by Portfolio,
a member of Penguin Group (USA) Inc.

1   2   3   4   5   6   7   8   9   10

Copyright © Geoff Colvin, 2009
All rights reserved

LIBRARY OF CONGRESS CATALOGING-IN-PUBLICATION DATA

Colvin, Geoffrey.
    The upside of the downturn : ten management strategies to prevail in the recession and thrive in the aftermath / Geoff Colvin.
        p. cm.
    Includes index.
    ISBN 978-1-59184-296-5
    1. Management. 2. Recessions. 3. Business cycles. 4. United States—Economic conditions–2001- I. Title.
    HD31.C6146 2009
    658.4'012—dc22   2009014871

Printed in the United States of America
Set in Adobe Caslon
Designed by Spring Hoteling

Contents

The Upside of the Downturn

CHAPTER ONE

The Greatest Opportunity

Why this historic downturn is so rich with possibilities

Lance Armstrong was trying to make history, but on the morning of Tuesday, July 20, 2004, he was by no means sure of succeeding. A lot was at stake. In the previous 101 years of the Tour de France, the world's greatest bicycle race, four men had managed to win it five times. No one had ever won it six times, and now Armstrong was going for his sixth victory. But on that morning Armstrong was not in the lead, and the race was mostly over. The Tour consists of twenty daylong stages, and after fourteen of them Armstrong was still behind Thomas Voeckler, a French rider who was looking formidable. He had inspired his country by remaining steadily in first place for the previous ten stages.

The next three stages would be raced in the Alps, so they would be extraordinarily punishing, even by the standards of the Tour. It has been called the world's most demanding sporting event, the equivalent of running several marathons a week for more than three weeks, but the mountain stages are so brutal that they are really like nothing else. So utterly draining is the effort required that the first time a true mountain stage was included in the Tour, in 1910, the winner crossed the finish line high up on the peak, staggered off his bike, and called the race organizers "assassins."

On that critical Tuesday morning, Voeckler began the first of the Alps stages, the fifteenth stage of the Tour, with a lead of twenty-two seconds over Armstrong. When the day ended, he was nine and a half minutes behind. Voeckler may have held the lead for ten consecutive stages, but when forced to climb into the Alps he suddenly performed in a radically different way. He placed fifty-fourth in that stage, ending his dream (and France's) for the year. He would never be in contention again. Armstrong was now in the lead but not yet in the clear.

The next day was harder because it included the most famous mountain in the Tour de France, a fearsome peak called l'Alpe d'Huez. The mountains encountered in the Tour are classed on a scale of difficulty from four, the easiest, to one, the hardest. But a few mountains are so difficult that they're given a special classification, a French phrase meaning "beyond categories," and l'Alpe d'Huez is one of these. With Voeckler out of the picture, Armstrong's main worry now was an Italian rider named Ivan Basso. "We take him very seriously," Armstrong had said a few days earlier. "We regard him as a threat." All the riders were being timed individually that day, and Armstrong, as the leader, was allowed to start last. He happened to start two minutes after Basso—yet he passed Basso on the way up the mountain and easily won the stage. Armstrong thus extended his lead, and Basso would not be a threat anymore.

In the last of the Alps stages the following day, the seventeenth stage of the race, two German riders still threatened Armstrong. Jan Ullrich was the 1997 Tour champion; he had lost narrowly to Armstrong in 2003 and was widely considered the primary challenger to him in 2004. Andreas Klöden had performed strongly throughout the whole race. Ullrich wasn't able to gain any ground that day, but Klöden made an audacious move at the very end, taking off in a sprint. With less than 600 yards to go, he was ahead of Armstrong by 110 yards, an apparently insurmountable lead. But Armstrong then stunned the crowd by finding reserves of power that no one had imagined. Roaring after Klöden—uphill—he crossed the line half a bicycle length ahead.

In just three transformative days, everything had changed. Three more stages remained in the 2004 Tour de France, but none would be in the Alps. For that reason, everyone who knew bicycle racing now understood that the race was over. Ullrich even told the media, after that seventeenth stage, that he, Klöden, and Basso would spend the rest of the race fighting one another for second place. While all the racers continued to compete hard during the following three days, they knew who would be riding down the Champs-Élysées in first place on Sunday. The race might not be officially completed, but Armstrong had already made history. His victory had been determined in the steepest mountains, in the few most brutally difficult portions of the race, and nothing that anyone could do in the flat, easy stages that followed would be able to change that.

This is, obviously, a story for our times. Performance in the Tour de France is a lot like performance in business and, for that matter, in virtuall y every realm: the worst, most difficult conditions bring out differences in competitors that were not previously apparent. Such conditions turn leaders suddenly into laggards and vice versa. They determine the winners and losers. Periods of extreme stress and challenge are reliably when dramatic competitive change takes place.

Research shows that the pattern holds emphatically in business. McKinsey recently examined how hundreds of high-tech companies performed during the severe tech recession of 2000–2002, for example. Of those that entered the recession as top performers, 47 percent had fallen out of that group by the time the downturn ended. Conversely, 13 percent of the previously mediocre-or-worse performers climbed into the top group during the recession. That's an industry-upending shift in the competitive order, and it all happened in a two-year period.

Today the whole world is economically in the Alps. More than just the Alps—we are in the mountains beyond categories. The terrible misery that people globally are enduring as a result is tragic, and nothing good can be said about it. But I hope it's clear also that for businesses and even for us individually, what many people regard as bad news—this is the hardest part of the race—can actually be good news. For this is that rare moment when we all face the greatest possible opportunity to make ourselves winners for a long time to come.

That opportunity is what this book is about.

Why This Opportunity Is So Attractive

It's easy to say that tough times are an opportunity, much harder for most businesspeople to find anything attractive in trouble on today's scale. A global economic decline that in many nations is already the longest since the Depression, that has wiped out trillions of dollars of wealth, thrown millions of people out of jobs, caused hundreds of thousands of businesses to close, is to most people just a mess, a curse, a plague. But in fact this historic downturn really does offer new, similarly scaled possibilities. The reasons are specific and hard-headed:

This downturn is worldwide, so your canvas of opportunity is huge. Not every country is in recession, but virtually all countries are affected powerfully, and they're facing widely diverse challenges. For example, Americans saved next to nothing during the economic boom from 2002 to 2007 and then, belatedly, began trying to put away more of their incomes. The Chinese, by contrast, are champion savers, and their government has actually begun urging them to save less and spend more. Now suppose you're a bank in the credit card business. In the United States you could offer a card that helps consumers pursue their newfound zeal for saving by rounding each purchase up to the next dollar and putting the difference into a savings account at your institution (which Bank of America has done), while in China you'd want to popularize the very concept of cards and get basic ones into the hands of lots of people—two huge opportunities.

It's the same in every business. All nations, all groups are challenged, each in a different way. Your opportunity to respond is broader than in the experience of any living person.

This downturn is severe and painful, answering the prayers of every business leader who wants to make big changes in his or her organization. Step one in every consultant's advice on how to lead change is "Create a burning platform." Often a leader will insist that the organization urgently needs to change for the future. But it's typically getting along okay at the moment and organizations resist change so strongly that mere exhortations can't get them to do things truly differently. Thus, the leader's challenge has generally been to manufacture a feeling of crisis. I know a former major CEO, still highly regarded, who was frustrated that his big, old industrial company wasn't changing as fast as he wanted. So he created a crisis through a bit of financial engineering, deliberately missing Wall Street's consensus earnings forecast by a penny a share—a miss that's widely regarded as a grave sign, because if the company couldn't find that last penny somewhere, things must be bad. The stock plunged, and the organization finally paid attention, though at tremendous cost to shareholders.

Hardly any CEO need resort to such tactics today. The platform really is burning. If ever people were ready to be led toward new ways of doing things, they are now. That's the meaning of the phrase we hear everywhere, first popularized by President Obama's team: "Never let a crisis go to waste." Just remember that every crisis eventually ends, so there's no time to lose.

This downturn is deep, meaning it's affecting people's most fundamental economic behaviors—spending, saving, borrowing, investing—in ways that may last for years. Consider basic attitudes toward homes, the places that carry the deepest psychological significance. (Home is mother, in case you were wondering.) America, Canada, Britain, Spain, Australia, and other countries have just gone through historic housing bubbles and busts. As a result, it may be a very long time before consumers in those nations again expect their homes to make them rich, a fundamental shift in attitudes that will alter the strategies of home builders, real estate agents, mortgage lenders, and many more players in that industry.

Millions of people worldwide are being traumatized by debt obligations that they can't meet, an experience that may reshape their feelings about borrowing for decades into the future. In the United States, the personal savings rate has been in decline since the early 1980s, but in this recession it has turned back up; does that trend presage a new attitude toward saving? Every company in financial services will have to reexplore the markets for loans and for savings vehicles. Consumption is also being transformed. Buy American, buy British, buy French, and buy Russian sentiment rose up quickly as the economy turned down; after years of focusing strictly on price and tangible product attributes, consumers may start to care much more deeply about which country's workers made a product and may do so for a long time, especially since unemployment tends to keep getting worse even after a recession ends.

Fundamental new consumer attitudes create opportunities for new kinds of businesses in every part of the economy. Such opportunities come along only rarely.

This downturn is long, which means that many companies won't survive it. The typical recession in most countries in recent decades has been short, usually less than a year. That's long enough to weed out only the weakest players. But this one is the longest since the Depression, which lasted forty-three months in the United States, and while it probably won't approach the magnitude of that one, it will be more than enough to clear out wide swaths of business. We've already seen the high-profile effects in investment banking and commercial banking, but they're only the beginning. In the media world, several major U.S. newspapers and many minor ones have closed, and they won't be coming back. Many famous retailers have failed, such as Circuit City and Mervyn's in the United States and Woolworth in the UK. In total about twenty-eight thousand businesses failed in the United States in the last prerecession year, 2007. More than twice that many will likely have failed in 2009.

The opportunity is to survive into the new world of fewer competitors and an economy that's growing again. Indeed, when executives are speaking to the media and can't think of any other basis for being upbeat, this is frequently what they say—that although they're being badly beaten up, good times are around the corner because so many competitors will disappear. Just make sure it's true. Angelo Mozilo, founder and CEO of Countrywide Financial—America's largest originator and holder of subprime mortgages—made exactly that point in telling CNBC why his firm would prevail. Of course it no longer exists, having fallen apart and been absorbed by Bank of America.

This downturn is novel, so most managers have never experienced anything like it and no one has an advantage in knowing how to manage for it. In the United States, for example, consumer spending rapidly declined more than in any recession since the Depression. No one in business today has ever had to respond to such a situation. Companies cut their dividends more in the fourth quarter of 2008 than in any quarter since Standard & Poor's started keeping track in 1956. In the UK, the Bank of England has cut interest rates to their lowest level in the bank's 311-year history. China is spending a $600 billion stimulus package, a venture into Keynesian economics previously unknown in the People's Republic. Around the world, no one has been here before.

Since no one has a head start in understanding how to respond, the advantage will go to those who work hardest now to see what is really happening in their business and industry and come up with bold, innovative responses for an unprecedented environment. Like what? Denny's, a casual restaurant chain, offered free breakfast to everyone in America—more than three hundred million people—on one particular day in February 2009; some two million showed up. The risk was obvious, but managers figured it was worth taking to send the message that we feel your pain, and by the way, we offer excellent value even when you do have to pay. A bonus benefit was that for at least a couple of days, the whole country was talking about this company at a time when businesses were finding it nearly impossible to get any favorable attention at all.

This downturn will test you personally, creating opportunities for growth and leadership that you have not faced before. Times of crisis present genuinely great opportunities not just to demonstrate leadership but also to develop it—to build leadership capabilities beyond what you or others in your organization now possess. Scientific research on great performance has shown persuasively that high abilities of all kinds are developed; they don't occur naturally. The question of whether great leaders are born or made is settled: they're made. The key to this development is pushing yourself—or being pushed—just beyond your current abilities, forcing yourself to do things you can't quite do. Companies that are famous for developing leaders—PepsiCo, Procter & Gamble, General Electric—are continually moving managers into jobs that accomplish exactly that. But the process is slow and can accommodate only so many people at any time.

The great thing about a financial crisis and a recession is that they offer everyone the opportunity to be stretched in their current jobs. Many CEOs, such as A. G. Lafley of P&G, have told me that being forced to manage through crises earlier in their careers—the Asian financial crisis in Lafley's case—built their abilities so effectively that it was critical to their becoming CEOs, that in fact they wouldn't have become CEOs otherwise.

Certain practices can make the experience especially productive. Coaching helps. Getting specific in your own mind about exactly which abilities you want to improve, and how, will turbocharge the results. But the main idea is that continually trying things you can't quite do is what makes you better, and doing it for a long time is what makes you great. And now, confronting the greatest business challenges to occur in generations, you're being handed a giant chance to become a great deal better. It's an opportunity that everyone faces but not everyone will grab.

Everyone is facing the opportunities that are present, though sometimes concealed, in the global downturn. Only a subset of businesspeople will recognize those opportunities. Of those people, only some will get past fear and defensiveness and even try to take advantage of the opportunities, and of that group only some will succeed. The winnowing is a merciless process, and getting all the way through it requires doing many things right. The foundation of them all is understanding first the very singular nature of this particular downturn.

CHAPTER TWO

The New Normal

The strange story of how we got here and what it means

Firefighting is the most dramatic form of responding to a crisis, so in this time of crisis it's worth considering what a group of psychological researchers learned when they studied firefighters. They investigated what two groups of firefighters, novices and veterans, actually saw when they looked at a burning building. The novices noticed the obvious features, the elements any of us would observe—the height and color of the flames, which parts of the building were involved. But the veterans, looking at the same fires, saw something different. They saw a story. They noticed the clues that told them how and where the fire had started, why it was burning as it was just now, and what it would likely do next. By seeing the fire as a story, not just a collection of traits, they could create a plan for managing it. That's what made them effective firefighters.

It's the same with the economy. Seeing the downturn as a bunch of statistics is easy, tempting, and almost useless. This recession is constantly talked about as some kind of freestanding event, but thinking of it that way won't help you manage it. Think of it instead as just one episode—a big, dramatic one—in a continuing narrative, a story without beginning or end. This episode will play out, and another will follow, very differently from what most people were expecting just a year ago.

Seeing the recession as part of a story is our only hope of understanding it well enough to manage through it. And as fascinating as the story is, what we all really care about is our own narrative—what happens to me and my organization in this story? That's what each of us will determine, and in doing so we will be writing the story as well as watching it. Every day we read about the vast financial forces at play, economies surging to and fro, trillions of dollars and millions of jobs, but it's important to remember that the story is actually about individuals like ourselves making decisions every day.

It's also important to focus on the story's most important elements, and in the current portion of the world's economic saga it's clear what they are. There are two. One is the behavior of American consumers. They're less than 5 percent of the world's consumers, but their massive spending power and, even more significant, their strange, unprecedented actions over the past several years have been critical in causing and shaping the recession.

The other main story element is risk and how economic players around the world have regarded it—a volatile love-hate relationship that is central to the story of the recession and what will come next.

The story of the world economy in recent years is infinitely complex, but it becomes a lot more comprehensible and useful if we think of it as a story about just those two elements: U.S. consumers and risk.

The Capital Wave

The story could be begun anywhere, since it has no beginning, but I think of a particular morning when the financial crisis was still just a vague suspicion and I asked Alan Greenspan why home prices had rocketed in the United States. He began his answer by talking about the fall of the Berlin wall. At first I thought maybe he had misunderstood me, but he hadn't. His point was that the end of communism marked the beginning of a global financial revolution that released huge quantities of capital into the world. Hundreds of millions of new capitalists in Eastern Europe and Russia, combined with billions of Chinese, whose own economic revolution was already under way, became productive workers, and they poured their savings into global capital markets. With the cold war over, government defense budgets shrank worldwide, so that much more capital was available than would have been otherwise.

The result was what Greenspan and his successor, Ben Bernanke, call the global savings glut: an ocean of capital such as the world had never seen, sitting in financial institutions and having to be lent to somebody. Much of it made its way to the United States, where its effect was multiplied by exciting new securitization vehicles invented by high-IQ finance specialists. One result of all that capital looking for a home was that essentially anyone could get a mortgage, including millions of people who never should have been allowed near one.

That version of the narrative, extremely compressed to this point, leaves out several important events. At just the time that communism was disappearing, in the early 1990s, the United States and other countries went through their first recession in eight years, a short and mild one in general. When it ended, the stage was set for one of the great bull markets of all time and, by the late 1990s, one of the largest corporate takeover waves ever—our first hint, well before the housing bubble, of how all that newly available capital could fuel markets in powerful ways. The world economy also staggered repeatedly, with financial crises in Mexico, Russia, and Asia, the collapse of Long-Term Capital Management, and finally the stock market crash of 2000, followed by the brief recession of 2001. That is, for about a decade after the savings glut started to build and roll around the world, the global economy never achieved nirvana. Something was always wrong somewhere.

But then the stars aligned as they had never done in history. The superabundance of capital accelerated as the supergrowth of China, India, and other savings-oriented economies released much more new capital into the world. At the same time, the improving efficiency of global capital markets meant that trillions of dollars were being continually directed to their highest-returning use worldwide, around the clock; each dollar of capital was working harder than ever. And the changing nature of the economy—based ever more on information, less on physical assets—meant that wealth could be created using far less capital than in the old industrial-based economy.

The result was more capital seeking a home than the world had ever seen—and when anything is that plentiful, it tends to be cheap. Interest rates were low and falling, especially as Greenspan kept lowering short-term rates to reinvigorate the economy after the 2001 recession—though as he always points out, he wasn't regulating the long-term rates that are most relevant to mortgage availability. Those rates were more affected by the global supply of capital.

Abundant capital by itself might not have changed the world, but something else happened at the same time, and the confluence turned out to be significant. Following the 2001 recession and the slow recovery of 2002, world economies boomed simultaneously. Nothing like it had ever happened before. Finally, after all the stumbles of the 1990s, everything seemed to be going right everywhere. From 2002 through 2007, all the world's major economies and most of the minor ones were growing at the same time, and at highly respectable clips.

Why Prosperity Became a Problem

It seems odd to say that worldwide economic prosperity could be a problem, but it became one when combined with the easiness of money. That mixture ignited a cycle of borrowing that eventually turned into trouble. Specifically, borrowers in the booming economic climate found that borrowing always seemed to work out. It cost little, and the assets bought with the borrowed funds kept rising in value—even assets like Miami condos, which were continually being bought by customers who intended only to resell them, not live in them.

Risk seemed to be evaporating. Jeremy Grantham, the well respected manager of the GMO mutual fund firm, calculated in 2006 that the risk-return relationship had actually turned upside down. That is, investors through history had always demanded a higher return for riskier investments, a practice so commonsensical that normally it's hardly worth mentioning. Yet in analyzing investments of all types globally, Grantham found "the first negative sloping risk-return line we have ever seen." Investors were paying such high prices for assets—modern art, junk bonds, London apartments, blue-chip stocks—that they were in fact accepting slightly lower returns from higher-risk investments.

Investors were willing to accept risk at no charge because the boom had lulled them into believing that risk might no longer even exist. So they borrowed and invested more, fueling the boom further—a self-reinforcing upward spiral. A successful private-equity manager told me with wonder in the midst of it all that a major bank was urging him to borrow $10 million to buy a painting; he, at least, realized it was madness. Yale economist Robert Shiller, like Grantham a lonely voice who tried to tell the world what was coming, observed that global economic growth picked up in the boom's final years for strictly circular reasons: "A good part of the extra growth since 2004 has probably been the increased spending caused by the speculative booms themselves."

In the world's largest economy, the United States, the cycle worked itself most powerfully in housing. That's significant because housing is the most valuable asset owned by consumers, who drive the U.S. economy and in large measure the world economy. For them, the logic of leverage was especially potent: as long as home prices were rising fast, consumers figured they must buy a home right now—otherwise they might never be able to afford one. They should buy the most expensive home they possibly could in order to get maximum benefit from rising values. And they should borrow as much money as anyone would lend them, again to reap maximum gain as their home rocketed in value. So millions of people did all those things, in the process pushing values even higher.

The momentously important result was that consumers felt rich and spent accordingly. They spent more every year, even when re-spectable economists argued that the party had gone on too long and they couldn't conceivably keep it up. Consumers dominated econo-mies worldwide as they hadn't done in decades. In the United States, consumption's share of total economic activity rose to 71 percent, the highest proportion since 1939. Buying—not saving or investing or paying taxes—became what economic life was all about, and the vast, global, consumer-powered machine just kept spinning faster.

The Day the World Changed

The day the world changed, though no one knew it at the time, was June 13, 2007. These turning points are never clear except in retro-spect, and no one can say exactly why they happen when they do. But on that day, for whatever reason, investors started waking up to risk, and all the world-changing turmoil we're coping with today has fol-lowed from that.

Specifically, investors began to feel they weren't getting paid enough for making risky investments. On the previous day, the yield on a ten-year U.S. Treasury bond, the world's safest ten-year invest-ment, was 5.3 percent, while the yield on an index of corporate junk bonds, representing some of the world's sketchiest financial instru-ments, was only 7.7 percent—an extraordinarily narrow spread for such a broad difference in risk. Indeed, it was the narrowest the spread would ever be. The next day, June 13, it began to widen, and it kept widening for a nearly incredible eighteen months.

At first the effects were barely noticeable, but by August they were unavoidable. That's when the subprime crisis began, for the simple reason that investors who had previously ignored the risks of subprime mortgages and the securities built from them were now demanding to be paid a more realistic—that is, higher—return. Bond yields and prices are opposite ends of a seesaw, so when yields rise, prices must fall. Thus, all the banks holding subprime debt found that these assets were suddenly worth much less than they had been just a few months before. With their assets evaporating, banks held ever less capital with which to support lending—and the great economic chill was under way.

The upward spirals of the boom slowed, stopped, and went into reverse, with all their self-reinforcing power now pushing down. Most important was housing and its effect on consumers. The value of U.S. homes had actually started falling more than a year earlier, in June 2006, but consumers hadn't much cared. Credit was still available. They could still get a mortgage easily or take out a home equity loan to finance a vacation, so the spending party rolled on. But now they couldn't, and that changed everything. Consumer confidence fell. Spending slowed way down. Consumers faced the new logic of falling home prices: instead of buying a home right now, it was smarter to wait; but if you were selling one, you'd better get it on the market immediately, before prices fell further. Of course, such behavior just pushed prices down more, making consumers feel even poorer and spend even less. In the final few months of 2007 consumers made one last desperate stab at maintaining their treasured lifestyles, borrowing heavily on the only source of funds they had left: credit cards. But the plastic-financed 2007 holiday season was the end of the party. Just six months after investors came to their senses about risk, the recession had begun.

Not Since Genesis

Every recession is unique, and this one is different in many ways, including the bizarre nature of the financial securities that got banks into trouble and its interconnected global complexity. But for people in business, the most important difference centers on the strange behavior of the protagonists of our story, consumers.

Ever since Joseph decoded Pharaoh's dream about fat cows and thin ones and delivered his policy response—save in the fat years to survive in the thin ones—consumers have followed that model. In good times they put away some of the abundance because they know they'll need it in bad times to come. Then, when the bad times hit, they spend some of what they've saved. That's what consumers have always done because it's so obviously prudent. But it isn't what they did this time.

For the first time since Genesis, consumers did everything backward. During the expansion from 2002 through 2007, the savings rate of U.S. consumers fell rather than rose. In mid-2005 it even went negative, and it stayed below 1 percent for most of the period until late 2008. Then, with the recession really taking hold, consumers again did the opposite of what they've usually done and increased their saving. As the economy shrank, the savings rate of U.S. consumers climbed well above 3 percent, then above 4 percent, the highest level in over a decade.

That is the reverse of how consumers behaved during the Great Depression, for example. The personal savings rate declined following the 1929 stock market crash, and in the Depression's two worst years, 1932 and 1933, the rate went negative—consumers spent more than they earned. When the economy improved, their savings rate (the percentage of disposable income saved) went back up, reaching 6 percent by 1937. When the economy then turned down in 1938, the rate dropped to 2 percent; the following year it rose. It was all a textbook illustration of logical saving behavior.

That pattern moderates business cycles. It stabilizes the economy by damping down spending during expansions and fueling it during recessions. But the reverse behavior makes cycles more extreme, and that's a major reason this recession is so bad. Consumers really do need to save more, but to get out of the recession they also need to spend more, and they can't do both at the same time, especially with jobs disappearing in huge numbers. It's a double whammy: not only do consumers lack savings to dig into and spend during this downturn, but they're also spending a smaller proportion of their incomes (which are themselves stagnating, so maybe it's a triple whammy). Put it all together and it's clear why this recession is so deep and so long.

The central mystery: Why did consumers go into hock in the fat years? One argument is that they were behaving rationally. As homes increased in value, they were doing people's saving for them, so people figured they didn't have to save out of current income. The trouble is that after home values turned down in mid-2006 and started making consumers poorer rather than richer, their savings rate kept right on falling. A related theory is that plunging savings rates reflected mortgage madness, as people who never should have been given a loan borrowed up to 100 percent of their home's value. But that explanation doesn't hold up either, because consumers were going heavily into most other types of debt as well. In fact, they were spending record proportions of their incomes just to service their personal debt—even with interest rates near historic lows.

Maybe it was just a mania, focused not on tulip bulbs or Internet stocks but on the simple joy of buying, reinforced by a belief that bad times were no longer inevitable. Americans hadn't seen a severe recession in twenty-five years; perhaps such things were now relics of history. Or maybe some critical mass of people had never known real privation; if you've never missed a meal in your life, why would you worry about thin cows?

The critical point is that consumers, like investors, had come to believe that risk had faded and maybe disappeared. That belief gave them the confidence to borrow when they should have been saving, and to spend like no people had ever spent before, just as financial institutions gained the confidence to lend more promiscuously than they ever had.

That's how this strange story has led to a recession of historic proportions. Now businesspeople need to know what will happen in the story's next episode.

The New Normal

Because this recession is so severe, and because of the unique way in which it happened, we can be sure that it will change the world in several big, long-lasting ways. The changes are already happening.

The structure of industries will change profoundly as various players disappear and others transform themselves. It happened first in financial services, where all of Wall Street's major investment banks either disappeared (Bear Stearns, Lehman Brothers, Merrill Lynch) or converted into commercial banks (Goldman Sachs and Morgan Stanley). The auto and life insurance industries are probably next in line, and the line is long. All players in the economy have been traumatized in ways that will change their attitudes and behavior.

We don't have to wait for the recession to end to see the new world that it's creating—to glimpse the next episode in the story. Specifically:

The U.S. economy will become less consumer driven and consumer focused. In the endless news coverage of the recession, we've been told repeatedly that consumption accounts for some 70 percent of the U.S. economy. That's true, but it wasn't always so. In any economy, all activity falls into just a few basic categories: personal consumption, investment, government spending, and the net of imports and exports. From the 1950s to the 1980s, consumption's share held remarkably steady at a much lower level, around 61 percent to 63 percent. In the 1980s it rose to around 67 percent and stayed there through the 1990s. Only in the shopping-fueled expansion that began in 2002 did it rise to 70 percent, hitting a high of 70.9 percent in the second quarter of 2008.

There's no reason the United States couldn't return to a more historically normal level of consumption. In fact, it's inevitable. Consumers in the near term will be forced to cut back, while government's share of GDP will grow. In the longer term, lenders that have been burned will be more careful about financing consumers, and consumers will be occupied for the next several years paying off the mountainous debts they accumulated in the boom.

Most economists thought consumers would be tapped out long ago. They proved far hardier than anyone imagined, but now that they're well and truly tapped out, it will be a long time before they're again as important as they recently were.

As the shopping fever cools, a large-scale, long-term pullback by U.S. consumers holds several further implications. The most important:

Social attitudes toward working, saving, spending, and borrowing will shift. Life would be simpler if people really behaved as we were taught in our introductory economics course, but they don't. People aren't economic machines, making rational calculations about price and utility at all times. They're swayed by cultural norms and social pressures, which are changing in reaction to the debt mania that led to the recession.

There's already evidence that the quaint notion of thrift is standing just offstage, ready to make a big entrance. Most consumers need to pay down debt but don't have many assets they can sell for that purpose, so their only solution is to spend less money. The Thrift Project, a research effort by several think tanks, has produced a recent report (*For a New Thrift: Confronting the Debt Culture*), a book, and a traveling exhibit. Ronald T. Wilcox, a professor at the University of Virginia's Darden School of Business, has written a book called

Whatever Happened to Thrift?: Why Americans Don't Save and What to Do About It. The common message: America's debt addiction has been seriously bad news for the country and needs to be fought.

Debt is a deeply cultural matter. Thrift used to be a virtue, a mark of character, debt an unfortunate necessity at best. The old days aren't coming back, but forces in today's society are already being adapted to clothe thrift in modern dress. One is environmentalism; the mantra "reduce, reuse, recycle" is a formula for saving money, while wasting resources not only is personally profligate, but also harms everyone by hurting the planet. In Hollywood a Prius is far hipper than a Hummer. Another culture-shaping trend is health-care and retirement anxiety; if you don't save enough to pay all your own bills, then you're forcing your kids and mine to pay them, and that's not right.

Such a cultural shift would affect virtually every company. For example, how often do you really need a new car? If consumers on average decided to drive an extra fifty thousand miles before trading in a vehicle—if driving a well-maintained ten-year-old car became cool rather than slightly shameful—the effect would be huge. An excellent year in the U.S. auto business used to be seventeen million vehicles sold. If the new normal is fourteen million, a vast industry that's already being transformed would be revolutionized.

Think also of financial institutions, retailers, restaurants, hotels, sellers of any other product or service—all will be affected not just by the economic force of the recession, but also more lastingly by the new attitudes it creates. Veterans of the Depression loathed debt all their lives and were terrified by the possibility of losing a job. Today's young workers, previously debt-happy and notorious job hoppers, may be similarly affected.

The world economy will become less U.S.-centric. If American consumers have driven the world economy, and their horsepower is considerably reduced, then businesses everywhere (including in the United States) will increasingly look elsewhere for growth. This is a long-term trend that the recession is accelerating. The nation that will become the world's main source of growth is, of course, China, and it will happen much sooner than most people expect. A prerecession study by the economist Angus Maddison, the preeminent scholar of international economic comparisons, projected that China would become the world's dominant economic superpower not in 2050, as expected several years ago, or in 2030, as we later thought, but in 2015. That projection assumed the U.S. economy would grow 2.6 percent a year on average, which no longer looks realistic. So maybe the handover will happen sooner.

When it does, America will close out a 125-year run as the world's number one economy. We assumed the title in 1890 from—guess who. The UK? France? Germany? No. The world's largest economy until 1890 was China. That's why Maddison says he expects China to "resume its natural role as the world's largest economy by 2015." It appears we Americans were just arrivistes who managed to elbow our way into the top spot for what seems like an eyeblink in China's four thousand years as a continuous culture.

Some of the implications of China's accelerated rise are clear. For companies: focus intensely on getting better at your highest-value activities. Just because the Chinese will be fighting you on that turf doesn't mean you'll lose. It only means you'll have to work harder to win. For individuals: you can avoid competition with Chinese workers by doing place-based work, which ranges in value from high (emergency surgery) to medium (specialized construction trades) to low (pouring concrete). But the many people who do info-based work, which is most subject to competition, will have to get dramatically better in order to be worth what they cost. For government leaders: improve U.S. education above all.

Playing a smaller role in the world economy isn't necessarily bad for the United States. Once global growth resumes, a richer world can be good for everybody. But a reduced presence will demand a new mind-set for managers, investors, and consumers everywhere.

Investors will remain spooked by risk for a long time. You'll recall that on the day before everything started changing, on June 13, 2007, a ten-year Treasury bond was yielding 5.3 percent, while an index of junk bonds yielded 7.7 percent. By the end of 2008, the yield on the Treasury bond was down to 2 percent; investors accepted this measly return because the bond was safe. By contrast, the junk bond index had risen to nearly 20 percent, and some junk bonds were yielding 40 percent; investors were now demanding a staggering return for bonds they regarded as dangerous. It was the most dramatic reversal of investor attitudes toward risk ever seen.

This new horror of risk is undoubtedly overdone, as wrong in one direction as the previous blithe acceptance of risk was in the other. But it may last for years, just as the earlier error did, because it carries its own unfortunate logic. As long as traumatized investors and lenders keep their capital in ultrasafe vehicles, the riskier investments that produce higher returns will be starved and get nowhere. Investors will thus feel confirmed in their choices and will keep their money in low-risk, low-return havens. That pattern won't last forever—it never does—but it won't end soon.

Government will play a much larger role. It isn't just the massive stimulus spending by the United States, China, Japan, Britain, Germany, and most other developed economies. Beyond the amounts being spent, these governments are deciding which industries and companies will receive billions of dollars and which won't. As banks and insurers verge on failure, many governments are only a step away from managing large parts of the financial sector. The governments of all these nations are imposing significant new regulation on businesses, and not only financial companies. Just as the rise of terrorism created a large new role for the security sector of government, this recession is creating a large and long-lasting new role for the regulatory sector.

In addition, all that stimulus spending will have to be paid for through taxes sooner or later. So government will also be imposing itself further into the business of extracting money from consumers and businesses. At the same time, governments will try to shield suffering constituents through protectionism. That will, of course, be terrible for the world economy, but the process is already well under way.

Culturally this is the reversal of the Hurricane Katrina effect. Then government looked incompetent while business rode to the rescue, with Wal-Mart, FedEx, Home Depot, and others sweeping in to offer victims well-organized help. *Fortune* magazine's cover line: "Government Broke Down. Business Stepped Up." Now the opposite is happening. Business looks inept or worse, and we turn to government to punish the guilty, help the suffering, and fix the economy. The new view: business screwed up; government steps in. Sir Martin Sorrell, chief of the giant WPP communications firm, told me, "Government is the only growth industry in the world right now."

For businesses there's no avoiding this new world, only embracing it and responding to it. You don't have to respond perfectly, just better and faster than your competitors. The best companies are responding in ten particular ways, all of which we'll examine. For every company, the important first step is the same. So that's what we look at next.

CHAPTER THREE

Reset Priorities

The critical first response to a radically new reality

Jamie Dimon is arguably the only major bank CEO who has come through the financial crisis so far looking good. As chief of JPMorgan Chase, he got the bank out of subprime mortgages in 2006 and kept it so financially strong that when other major institutions failed—notably Bear Stearns and Washington Mutual—Chase bought them and their still-valuable assets for minimal prices. That's why, after more than a year of continuing disasters in the financial world, Chase is often called the last bank standing. Now everyone wants to learn more about how Dimon manages, and he's not bashful about explaining it. When a Harvard Business School professor asked him, in October 2008, how he was managing through the crisis, Dimon was perfectly clear about what was most important: "You have to prioritize. I am shocked at the number of people who are watching that train coming down the track"—meaning the recession—"and they're still worrying about their strategic plan for 2009. We canceled all that stuff—*all of it*—meetings, travel, you name it, to focus on the fact that we're in the middle of a real crisis."

Dimon was describing something that consultants call a head nodder—you say it and everybody nods their heads in agreement—yet as he observed, many companies find his actions almost impossibly difficult to imitate. In good times, the whole organization becomes aligned with goals based on assumptions about favorable conditions. When those conditions radically change, everything the organization is doing has to be rethought, and much of it must be altered. That's difficult for obvious organizational reasons. Changing the direction of even a small business can feel like turning an aircraft carrier. More important, as we'll see a bit later, are the extremely deep psychological reasons why we all have trouble responding fast and in the best way to suddenly changed conditions; understanding those reasons is a big help in overcoming our reluctance to change.

Hard data confirm what Dimon noticed about managers just not wanting to face the most overwhelming change in economic reality in seventy-five years. A survey of managers worldwide by Booz & Company, a management consulting firm, conducted in December 2008, found that many of the hardest-hit companies were not accelerating their efforts to preserve cash, which is reliably one of the most critical moves such companies must make in a recession (if they do it right; see Chapter 7). Large numbers of respondents seemed to believe they were facing reality but were unrealistically hopeful about its effect on them—a common response. For example, more than half of respondents in every region of the world believed their own company would emerge from the recession stronger than it was going in; obviously, some of them are going to be wrong.

Speculating on why so many managers seemed unwilling to face the new reality, the Booz researchers wrote, "The speed of the downturn may have left people in shock—unable, for the moment, to take the most appropriate action." The shock effect is a possible explanation, but inability to act in the early stages of a crisis is a common problem, which Dimon diagnosed insightfully from his position in the midst of the storm: "A lot of people don't have the ability to act. A lot of the actions you take in the middle of a crisis like this are admissions of your own failure—we bought X, we're gonna sell it, we're gonna take a loss, we have to tell the shareholders. People don't want to tell the shareholders, don't want to admit they're wrong, so they sit there—and these problems don't age well." That is, reluctance to admit failure in the early stages means you'll probably be forced to admit a much larger failure later.

The Booz researchers suspect another reason may explain why so many businesspeople don't want to face reality: "Some executives may be waiting for additional data—hoping that the downturn will turn out to be less severe than their gut instincts are telling them." No doubt it's true. We've all seen analysis paralysis, postponing a decision on the pretext of trying to make a better decision but generally doing just the opposite. Waiting for more data is usually an act of desperate self-delusion, a willful silencing of what your inner voice is trying to tell you. The inner voice is almost always right.

None of the other strategies for managing in this recession will work until this one—facing the new reality and resetting priorities—has been fully pursued. It's the first fundamental. Jack Welch was fond of saying, "Confront reality—not as you wish it were, and not as it used to be, but as it is." That doesn't mean just acknowledging the latest economic statistics. It means bringing them home. GDP is shrinking, consumer spending is down, home foreclosures are up—but what does it all mean for your firm? What's your specific new reality?

The changes in your reality are probably much more extensive than you realize. To grasp them fully, examine how your company's world has changed in six key categories that shape performance—and viability:

Financial strength. Since this recession started as a financial crisis—which is not the way most recessions start—its effect on a company's finances demands special attention. The disruptions that showed up first in the financial sector were shocking and illustrate how life-threatening the new financial reality can be. For example, the idea that AIG would ever—ever—be less than a rock of financial stability was simply unimaginable, right up until the end. In fact, on the very day the U.S. government effectively took it over, AIG still had a strong investment-grade credit rating. Not long thereafter, investors even got nervous about General Electric, then a triple-A-rated firm and still one of the most profitable companies on earth; the price of credit default swaps on GE debt—basically insurance against default—suddenly jumped by a factor of ten, apparently because investors felt they didn't know enough about GE's giant financial business, GE Capital.

The effects almost immediately spread into the larger economy worldwide, as banks that weren't certain of their own financial condition cut back on lending. Dunkin' Brands, owner of the Dunkin' Donuts and Baskin-Robbins chains, has always helped franchisees get financing but in the new environment found that many big national banks could no longer be relied on; it turned to financially solid regional banks instead.

At least Dunkin' was able to find credit for its franchisees. The crisis terrified many bankers and investors out of the market completely, so that other firms have been unable to find credit anywhere at any price. The commercial paper market practically shut down for a time; McKesson, the huge pharmaceutical distribution company, was one of many firms suddenly locked out, though it carried on with bank lines of credit.

In assessing its new financial reality, every company must now ask: What is our access to capital? If it stays like this, how long can we continue? What new sources of capital can we find? If we had to sell assets to raise capital—now, at the worst possible moment to sell assets—what could we get for them? How can we reduce our capital requirements? How can we reduce working capital? Will our cost of capital likely rise as lenders and investors worry about risk, or fall as central banks cut interest rates?

Answering those questions is vital because the answers will paint a picture that's markedly different from what it was just a year ago. **Competitive advantage.** Has the recession changed your standing versus competitors? It can happen in all kinds of ways. Most obvious and dramatic is when significant competitors disappear, as is happening in banking (IndyMac, Washington Mutual), magazines (*PC Magazine*, *Men's Vogue*), retailing (Linens 'n Things, KB Toys), and many other sectors. But this recession can help or harm your competitive position on many other dimensions as well.

The worsening economy can pit you against companies that you didn't previously regard as competitors. For example, five-star hotels are cutting prices as lots of travelers decide they can sleep just as soundly in a midrange hotel, forcing those categories to compete against each other much more than before. The same phenomenon—top-end competitors realizing they must now compete with lower-priced players, and vice versa—is happening in autos, retailing, and plenty of other industries. The change requires everyone to play a new competitive game. The Four Seasons in your city is competing not just against the Mandarin Oriental but also against the Travelodge. The chief of Travelodge, Guy Parsons, believes the recession is revolutionizing his business as well-to-do travelers try his hotels for the first time. Already, he told a London magazine, he sees guests at his two Covent Garden properties—where rooms are as little as twenty-nine pounds a night—leaving in tuxedos and ball gowns to attend the nearby opera or ballet.

Overall demand can shift radically. We all like to believe that our customers can't live without our product or service, but a bad recession is when we find out if it's really true. Early in this recession, the conventional view was that the richest consumers would be unaffected, so demand for luxury products would hold steady while goods sold to the middle class would suffer. In reality, those luxury products are entirely discretionary—no one actually needs a Harry Winston diamond or a Bentley Continental Flying Spur—and their sales have been pounded.

Your cost advantage or disadvantage can change. In a recession as volatile as this one, the particular structure of your costs is more important than ever. Do you have long-term supply contracts? Should you? Are your costs hedged? Those are critical questions. Southwest Airlines has for years used hedging to manage its fuel costs, and in general the strategy has worked well. It was especially successful in the first half of 2008, as oil prices spiked to $147 a barrel while Southwest had locked in costs well below that level. But in the year's second half, when the recession sapped demand and the price dropped to less than $40 a barrel—much lower than Southwest or virtually anyone else had expected—the hedging strategy backfired. Southwest had locked in costs that were higher than the market price and higher than what competitors were paying. The airline lost hundreds of millions of dollars as a result.

Your talent advantage can change. More CEOs left their jobs in 2008 than in any year since the outplacement firm Challenger Gray & Christmas began tracking such things a decade ago. That's no surprise. In a severe recession plenty of CEOs will get fired, as they were at Citigroup, Merrill Lynch, Borders Group, Tyson Foods, and many other firms, or will decide on their own that it's a perfect moment to retire. The question for you is whether the change to a new leader is good news or bad news.

Government intervention. A recession this bad leads inevitably to a greater government role in business than we've seen since the Depression. The trend holds worldwide. It's clearest in the rapidly increasing cases of direct government ownership stakes in big, important companies such as major banks and insurers—yet executives in those companies clearly didn't appreciate how fully their world had changed as a result. Suddenly every expenditure they made had to pass the test of whether it was something appropriate for taxpayers to be funding. That's obviously no way to run a business— sometimes taking good customers on junkets to shoot partridges or attend a concert in Las Vegas makes sound financial sense—but it doesn't matter. Purely for the sake of appearances, Citigroup had to cancel a contract to buy a private jet, though canceling may have cost more than taking delivery. That's part of its new reality.

Far more numerous are companies that will be affected by new regulations. New rules are coming first in industries at the recession's epicenter—banking, mortgage lending, mortgage brokering, credit derivatives—but will follow quickly in other industries. New rules in the auto industry alone, as part of government support not only in the United States but also in Europe and Asia, will keep thousands of lawyers and accountants fully employed for many years. Similarly, we can expect governments to be more active in antitrust enforcement. That shift was a certainty in the United States when Obama's team replaced Bush's more laissez-faire administration, but it will likely happen worldwide also as regulators take a more skeptical view of all business activity.

How will multitrillion-dollar global stimulus programs in the United States, Europe, China, Japan, and elsewhere affect you and your competitors? Most of that money will be paid to companies. Who will get this historic bonanza of government contracting and who won't? The process of fighting for it isn't pretty, but losing this business to your competitors could be even worse. In several industries—construction, energy, education, water, broadband, and others—this will be one of the most important elements of the new reality over the next few years.

Government intervention will also take the form of protectionism, a lose-lose development that will make the world poorer—but it's happening anyway. America's giant stimulus program includes "buy American" requirements for iron, steel, and manufactured goods. The European Union is imposing duties on some forms of Chinese steel. Russia recently raised import duties on cars. That's just the beginning. The wave is building, and every company must determine whether it's a winner or a loser as a result.

The state of your customers. Your company is only as healthy as your customers, and their condition may be changing fast in this environment. The effect on their spending is not always simple and one-dimensional. For example, Wal-Mart, the world's largest retailer, has performed well in this recession, but in the summer of 2008 it was suffering. That's because most of its customers live paycheck to paycheck, and when oil went over $140 a barrel their gasoline bills swamped their ability to buy other things—but not all other things. At that time, I asked Doug McMillon, who was then CEO of Wal-Mart's giant Sam's Club division, to explain what was happening. He outlined the effect:

> Take gas off the top, and what it costs to heat the home as another big drag on the wallet, and then food inflation of 4 percent to 5 percent, which is a big number for the average U.S. consumer. So you'll see a bigger portion of the check going toward energy and food and less on things like electronics—though they'll still have the coolest cellphone as they prioritize those discretionary purchases. We're still selling a lot of flat-panel televisions.

Customer spending dynamics changed further when oil prices plunged—good news—but unemployment jumped—bad news. For other companies, different factors will be more important. If you sell any kind of capital good—cars to consumers, bulldozers to construction companies, power turbines to electric utilities—then your customers' ability to get credit is centrally important and probably much changed from a year ago. In general, this is a time when companies need to gauge customer health much more closely and frequently than before.

Your reputation. Long before this recession, corporate reputation was becoming more economically valuable than it had ever been previously. Consumers increasingly consider a company's reputation when they make buying choices, which is one reason that investors are now more likely to shun companies with poor or declining reputations. The phenomenon is more advanced than many people realize. One of America's most prestigious law firms, Akin Gump Strauss Hauer & Feld, now has a "reputational recovery" practice. An insurance broker, Lockton and Lloyd, offers reputation insurance: "When a data breach is followed by adverse media attention, the Data Breach Reputation Guard element of the policy will reimburse a business for reputational harm."

How is your company's reputation holding up in this recession, and what is the financial impact? Realize that your reputation may be affected by events having nothing to do with your company or its behavior. In the developed economies, any firm connected with investment banking or commercial banking is probably suffering—even firms that never touched subprime mortgages, hold no toxic assets, and continue to lend. One of the more striking social phenomena of recent times is that absolutely no one wants to admit to being a banker, a sure sign of reputational damage.

A clear-eyed view of your firm's reputation today is a vital element of your new reality.

Your risks. Each company's new reality in this recession consists not just of changing levels of risk, but also of completely new risks. I asked Tom Neff, the Spencer Stuart headhunter who recruits CEOs and board members for the world's largest companies, about the new demands on boards, and his response applies to managers at all levels:

> Boards have to spend more time thinking about the unthinkable—scenarios that would have seemed irrational, maybe unimaginable, just a year ago. What if our lead bank disappears? What if we have a liquidity crisis? What if the Dow goes to six thousand? What if our stock keeps dropping and attracts raiders?
>
> The other subject that boards need to focus on more is

enterprise risk management. It's not just risk in the sense that banks need to focus on it, but what are the risks in our business model, what are the global risks that could affect our business? It's a holistic approach to the subject, and stress testing what we're doing.

This recession is certainly increasing risks of the traditional type, such as financial leverage (high debt levels) and operating leverage (high breakeven points), plus risks in the areas described above, such as reputation and customer health. Most companies know how to analyze those risks. What's new this time, and requires new analytical skills, is the risk to your firm posed by failure of the financial system: you could feel confident that all your risks are well understood and controlled yet still be damaged by a system failure that neither you nor anyone else contemplated. That's a large part of what caused the plunge in GE's stock, for example. The challenge for everyone now is to identify the larger systems to which your company is exposed—capital markets, insurance, data, infrastructure— and imagine ways in which they might fail and what that would mean for you.

Making Smart Decisions Under Stress

Understanding all the elements of your new reality is a big job, but the great thing about doing it is that it creates a picture—a rich overall view of your business in today's new environment. Looking at that big picture, you'll probably realize that many of your prerecession goals just aren't realistic anymore. Growing 15 percent? Opening a hundred new stores in the United States? Expanding into Vietnam? Abandoning such goals for now isn't failure; it's facing reality and protecting the business. In their place you'll create new goals— increasing market share, lowering breakeven points, creating new customer value propositions, and others—that will serve you better and will be the subjects of later chapters.

But in a way, this analysis, this assessment of the new reality and revising of goals, is the easy part. The hard part is responding— getting yourself and others to embrace the new reality, make decisions in a stressful, fast-changing, and uncertain environment, and take action. The reasons that's so hard are deep-seated in all of us. Understanding those reasons is key to getting past the difficulties and operating in the new environment faster and more effectively than your competitors.

 "Substandard performance by decision-makers in crisis situations is particularly common," said Daniel Frei of the University of Zurich. He studies international crises at the government level, but his observation is just as apt when applied to business. What goes wrong is no mystery. Psychologist James Thompson has spotted three ways people blow decisions when the pressure is on, and most of us have seen all of them at work:

- People obsess about insignificant problems and ignore what's important. Maybe that's because the real problem seems frighteningly large or just impossible to handle. The danger is especially acute today because this global recession is the largest problem that most people in business have ever encountered. The temptation to delude oneself will be greater than ever.

- Their perceptions become distorted. Whatever you're focused on becomes bigger and more important in your perception, so if you're focused on insignificant details, you'll miss what really matters. If you aren't looking for something, you may not see it, and in today's environment we're all especially vulnerable to looking in the wrong place.

- They insist on proving that their mistaken hypothesis about the situation is actually correct. Everyone in business wants to do a good job, but self-preservation is a much deeper and more powerful urge. We'd all rather prove we were right than admit we were wrong, and that tendency can persist past all reason. It happens in business all the time. Ken Olsen, founder of Digital Equipment Corporation, famously dismissed the personal computer in its early days with the memorable remark, "Why would anyone want a *personal* computer?" When it soon became clear that millions of people wanted one, he kept trying to show that he was right and they were all wrong. Digital faltered, was bought by Compaq, and disappeared.

Other researchers have figured out how stress hijacks the brain's ability to work. A little stress is good—it increases focus. But beyond a certain point, stress activates a part of the brain called the amygdala, which stores emotional memories, and clear thinking becomes virtually impossible. That crossover point varies by individual, but the stress levels in this recession can become so high that almost no one will be immune.

Closely related is the effect of uncertainty. "People abhor decision making under significant uncertainty because they'll look dumb," Richard Zeckhauser, a professor at Harvard's Kennedy School of Government, once explained to me. That's a bigger problem than it may seem. Looking dumb—or thinking that's how you look—can trigger a downward spiral of deteriorating performance. "I'm a serious bridge player," he said, "and I've noticed that people do worse after bad outcomes." That makes no sense, of course: "They should forget about it—it's sunk costs." But it happens anyway, and since bad outcomes are everywhere in this recession, this effect threatens to harm the performance of virtually every company.

The danger is that with the global economy in turmoil, lots of people in your organization are caught looking as if they made big mistakes. Inside the organization and perhaps publicly, they are already charged with errors. Never mind that virtually no one imagined how broad or fast this economic collapse would be. The downward spiral of performance could lead to worse decisions down the road.

How to respond? The best and clearest explanation comes from studies of the military, where stress is worst and the consequences most serious. Research by the World Health Organization has shown how soldiers avoid the harmful effects of the stress and uncertainty of combat. Note how each factor has a clear parallel in business.

Soldiers avoid the effects of combat stress and uncertainty when

- **They feel in control.** We can never promise our colleagues that the world won't jump up and bite them unexpectedly. In a large sense, that's what has just happened. But we can show them that we're not entirely at the mercy of events. Leaders need to explain—probably in much more detail than during normal times—what the company must achieve in order to survive and thrive, and then see that each person understands his or her role in making it happen. A crucial distinction is that people don't need to be promised success; they know such a promise is unrealistic. They just need to know what they can do, within their own authority and ability, that will best help the company succeed and protect their own jobs.
- **They have strong group cohesion.** One of the best-established precepts in military life is that no soldier goes into combat for his country. He goes in for the guys on either side of him. The analog in business is that people don't get up and go to work in the morning to make the share price go up. They do it because they believe that they

and their team are doing something good. Group cohesion is built over time, and if a company doesn't have it, now is a little late to start building it. But it's also true that nothing gets people to bond like shared adversity, and most organizations are sharing a lot of it now. For companies that need more group cohesion, this is the perfect moment to encourage it, perhaps by making rewards contingent on overall group performance. (We'll look more closely at pay practices in the next chapter.)

- They trust their leaders. Trust is slowly won and quickly lost, so it's tough for companies to do much about this in the near term after trouble hits. A particular challenge in this recession is that so many leaders are changing, and in most cases employees are especially suspicious—that is, not especially trusting—of the new leader. It's well established that the only way for a leader to build trust is to make and keep commitments, so it's important not to make commitments that aren't ironclad. You may not want to say, "I promise not to close the Springfield plant." But you may be able to say, "If the Springfield plant achieves a quality level of X this quarter, I promise to pay every employee a special bonus of Y." And then be sure to do it.

- They have high motivation. This can be achieved in many ways. One of the strongest is a record of success—people who feel they're succeeding are powerfully driven to succeed again. The opportunity for companies is greater than it may seem, because most companies do a terrible job of telling employees about corporate successes. No organization is perfect, but every organization has victories that all employees should know about. Especially in a serious downturn, the value of publicizing successes within a company is tremendous.

- They feel well armed and protected. In business that means having excellent products to sell, effective marketing, appealing value propositions—in circumstances like that, everyone in the company can face the world with confidence. If you don't have those things, there's no substitute for the hard work of developing them. You can't fool the employees, who invariably know more than the leaders about such matters.

- They feel well trained. Again, reality is what counts: *Are they well trained?* It's amazing how many companies cut training and development in a recession. In a world where human capital is more valuable than any other asset, it's foolish. Many managers may not appreciate this additional danger, that in a bad recession, employees who lack training will feel more stressed and uncertain and will make worse decisions.

- They have a reliable medical corps. No one expects that a historic recession will be without casualties. What employees need to know is that if they lose their jobs, they'll be well looked after—will have excellent outplacement counseling, continued medical benefits for a substantial period, fair severance pay. Research has shown that one of the strongest influences on the loyalty of employees is what they see happening to colleagues who get laid off. The reasoning is simple: if the company won't take care of me, then I certainly won't try hard to take care of the company. At a time when most companies are laying off employees, exactly how it's done is an opportunity to influence the performance of those who remain.

All of those factors that reduce stress are likely to weaken rather than strengthen in a recession. That's why it's especially important to give them extra attention. Overstressed decision makers are bad decision makers, so unless the stress problem is at least blunted, nothing else will turn out well.

Forming a clear picture of your business's new reality, and then understanding the challenges of acting on what you see, is the crucial first step toward finding opportunities in this recession. Those opportunities will arise in every aspect of your business. But in what we've learned so far you may have noticed a continuing emphasis on human capital. That's because it's irrefutably clear that the most influential factor in the success of any company today is its people—their knowledge, abilities, relationships, and development. Certainly lots of other factors are important, and we'll investigate opportunities in strategy, operations, finance, and other areas. What counts most is beyond doubt, however, and this recession, more than any in decades, is revolutionizing the relationship between companies and workers.

Up to fifty million jobs could be lost worldwide by the end of 2009, says the International Labor Organization, part of the United Nations. Yet the people who hold those jobs have not decreased in value. On the contrary, the global supply of ingenuity, passion, inspiration, and human energy is at least as great as it ever was. That's a major reason why this recession is a massive opportunity for wise companies to increase the value of their human capital. It's the topic we examine next.

CHAPTER FOUR

Protect Your Most Valuable Asset

It's your people—yet they're often valued the least

General Motors eliminated more than 20,000 jobs in 2008 and announced plans to get rid of an additional 47,000 jobs as part of its plan for being rescued by the U.S. government. Ford and Chrysler also laid off thousands. The Detroit Three have eliminated more than 140,000 factory jobs since 2005 and have made clear that many more thousands of employees will have to go if these companies are to survive.

Toyota, as of this writing, has not laid off any employees or announced any plans to do so. In fact, Toyota has never laid off anyone. It's not that Toyota was still selling as many cars and trucks in 2009 as it was 2007. On the contrary, its sales were whacked more heavily than at any time in the company's history, though not nearly as badly as the Detroit Three's sales were hit. Nor was the company continuing to turn out millions of vehicles and storing them unsold on some vast parking lot. Instead, Toyota was doing what it has always done in recessions: continuing to pay workers, who continue to come in to work every day. If they aren't needed to make cars all day, which in this environment they often aren't, then they do other things. They take classes in workplace safety or how to handle materials. They participate in exercises, developed at Toyota over many years, on how to improve productivity. They go to seminars on diversity or ethics. They go through assessment exercises to see how much they're learning.

Toyota doesn't promise its employees that it will never lay anyone off. The company recently recorded the first loss in its seventy-year history, and in a recession of the current magnitude it wouldn't be surprising if this firm, like others, has to do things it never previously had to do. It has already offered buyouts to eighteen thousand U.S. employees, which is a first. But regardless of whether this historic downturn forces Toyota to make its first layoffs, note a few significant points:

Its policy of keeping employees on staff during recessions and giving them extra training means that when the economy turns up, those employees are in the plant, ready to go, and probably far better prepared than the employees of any competitor.

Those employees are tremendously loyal to their employer. They are not only well equipped to be productive—they want to be productive. That second factor is at least as important as any other in how productive they really are.

The communities in which Toyota operates are also hugely loyal to the company. The advantages of being embraced by communities and their governments, rather than scorned by them, show up in myriad ways.

Toyota is a publicly traded corporation. Its stock is down by about half from its all-time high and is up slightly over the past ten years, as of this writing. Managers at big companies often object that people practices like Toyota's are simply not realistic for them because the stock market would murder them for such profligate spending. But apparently it isn't so. While Toyota's stock has suffered in this recession, it has declined no more than the overall market—and has far outperformed the shares of other carmakers. For comparison, consider that GM stock is down about 97 percent from its all-time high and trades for less than it did sixty years ago, as of this writing. Managers also object that they just can't afford to be as generous as Toyota and that it's unfair to suggest otherwise. Toyota, they note, is the world's largest car company and financially rock solid, with a triple-A credit rating. Of course such a company can be nice to its employees during tough times. Obvious question: which is the cause and which the effect? To ask the question is to answer it: each factor—Toyota's employee strategy and its financial success—clearly helps cause the other in a virtuous circle.

It's clear that Toyota's people practices during recession aren't some kind of nice perk. Rather, they're central elements of a strategy that has produced one of the largest, most successful, most stable companies on earth.

The New Importance of Human Capital

The first thing we all think of when a recession hits is the effect on employees. It's a direct connection in our brains: recession—people get fired. Despite the performance and practices of great companies like Toyota, sometimes a company truly cannot avoid getting rid of workers. Maybe the company was badly managed in the good times; for example, there's no longer any point in lecturing GM about the virtues of Toyota's system, because the way GM was managed over the past several decades means it simply cannot behave like Toyota now. Maybe the recession literally wipes out a company's business, or the business is still small and weak. The reality is that for all kinds of reasons, sometimes layoffs genuinely cannot be avoided.

But the best companies and best leaders take a larger view of their people during a downturn. They avoid the reflexive responses that they may have grown up with and that may be traditional in their own company. When they stop and examine today's environment, they find that it's full of opportunities—to begin practices they always should have been using, to improve the quality of their people, to increase employees' loyalty and motivation, to build the culture. The best companies will emerge from this recession as better places to work, stronger magnets for great people, and more formidable competitors in their industries.

The big danger is that most business leaders will respond to this recession with the wrong people practices, because the nature of the economy and of business success has changed so significantly since the last bad recession. Remember, in much of the world it has been some twenty-five years—two or three generations of management—since a really serious downturn. One of the largest changes in business during that time, arguably the largest of them all, is the role of human capital as the foundation of the world economy. Twenty-five years ago we were still a manufacturing-based world, which meant that physical assets were the most expensive pieces of capital that managers had to worry about. Every manager mouthed the words about the importance of people, but capital equipment was at the world economy's center, and physical stuff is what the economy primarily produced.

That was reality the last time business leaders had to respond to a recession anywhere near as large as today's. Everyone liked to have good people, but their role was to make the machines run.

We all know how profoundly that situation has changed, yet when it comes to people decisions in a deep recession, many managers obey ancient instincts from the industrial age. Intellectually they must know it's a new world. Financial results have long shown that companies are producing much more wealth with fewer physical assets. By the late 1990s Alan Greenspan was able to say, based on troves of data that are presumably available only to a Fed chairman, that America's GDP weighed no more than it had fifty years earlier, yet it was worth five times as much in real terms. No longer was it the role of people to make the equipment run. Now the role of equipment was to enable the people.

The continuing challenge, more difficult than it seems, is to manage the business according to that new reality. Most companies still don't do it very well, but this recession presents them with an excellent opportunity to catch up on moves they should have made long ago.

A Great Time to Develop and Train

The most fundamental move is to manage the development and evaluation of people much more actively. This is one of those head nodders that everyone agrees on, yet it doesn't happen in most companies because of cultural inertia. Most employees have always been responsible for their own development, and as long as the business was getting along acceptably, that routine was hard to shift. Similarly, evaluations at most companies, if they happen at all, are infrequent, stiff, and superficial, dreaded by both parties; altering that deeply entrenched pattern will never be easy without some outside motivation.

Now that motivation is here, and it offers more benefits than one may first realize. A deep financial crisis is obviously and undeniably a spur for change in how the business is run. An announcement that the company is going to get much more serious about developing employees just might be met with less eye rolling and more seriousness than it would be in other circumstances. What's more, it might even be met with some enthusiasm. We mustn't lose our heads: in many companies a stronger focus on how people are developed and evaluated will be seen cynically as a prelude to firing lots of them, and those companies face trust issues that will take a long time to resolve. But it's also possible that in a major recession, when employability becomes a top concern, people might be glad to hear that they're going to be developed a bit more thoughtfully and deliberately than they have been.

Development needn't mean classes and seminars. At many companies the most valuable improvements in development would involve something much simpler: a series of candid conversations between employee and boss specifically about how the employee could get better, some goals to strive for, and a plan for getting there. This approach is free. It's effective—it makes almost everyone better. And in a recession, unlike virtually any other time, everyone is powerfully motivated to make it work.

The other critical part of this system is frequent, rigorous evaluations. Again, they cost nothing. And in today's circumstances both parties are motivated like never before to take the process seriously—the evaluator because he knows he may eventually have to make a decision about whether this employee stays or goes, and the employee because he knows the same thing.

This isn't recession managing. It's just managing. At great companies—Procter & Gamble, Nokia, McKinsey—the process is an ingrained part of everyday life. The big opportunity for most other companies is to use the intensity of these times to get the process embedded in their corporate lives for the long run.

That's a start, and following those basic practices will substantially help any organization. But you can go further. In this recession companies are predictably slashing what they spend on more formal training and development. The cuts are the most severe in at least a decade. It's a classic pattern: when times turn tough, companies immediately cut travel and entertainment, advertising, and training and development. But in today's economy more than ever, cutting that last category is senseless. Not only is business more reliant on human capital than ever before, but your most valuable employees—especially the best young employees—demand that their employers develop them. It may well be that you need to lose some employees, but you want to lose the least valuable, not the most valuable (a topic we'll focus on shortly). Your best people are probably the most grateful for continued formal training and development. Bill Weldon,

CEO of Johnson & Johnson, one of the world's strongest and most admired corporations, says a critical job for the company now is "helping the employees recognize that we're going to continue to invest in them and their development."

In addition, continuing to offer training—adapted to the new environment—can help a company gain competitive advantage in the downturn. After all, in this changed world the requirements facing many of your people have probably changed also. The whole business will benefit if employees get help on how to deal with the evolving market. For example, Trane, the big (and for our purposes felicitously named) maker of heating, ventilation, and air-conditioning equipment, reported that rather than cut training in this downturn it was redirecting it to help sales and marketing people sell more services and cross-sell equipment. Any company could adapt in a similar way.

They'll Never Forget What You Do Now

More broadly, a recession is a large opportunity for a company to be a hero to its people. Shortsighted companies don't think about that; they figure every employed person is grateful just to have a job these days, so why worry about trying extra hard to please them? Better companies understand there's a reason. Any major event sparks a re-action, and part of the reaction to this recession is a rise in union membership and in government regulations to protect workers. Union membership in the United States actually rose in 2008 after decades of decline, a clear response to the slowing economy. Now, we could have a rich discussion about the large-scale pluses and minuses of labor unions, but I don't know of a single nonunionized company that really wishes its employees would all join a union. Right now especially is the time to make sure they don't feel the need to. That's a precept that some of the world's most successful, stable, admired (and largely nonunion) companies, such as FedEx, Toyota, and Walt Disney, have held to through recessions going back many decades.

Even if unions aren't an issue in your business, the same principle applies, and it's actually one of the largest principles in all of recession managing. This downturn may last a long time, but it will end, and when it does, everyone—not just employees but also customers, suppliers, investors, and regulators—will remember how your company behaved in the dark days. It may well be that even your best employees are in no position to go elsewhere right now. But they will not forget what kind of company their employer showed itself to be when the chips were down, and if they didn't like it, they'll be the first ones to bolt when the upturn arrives. That is, in fact, a classic pattern from past recessions: when good workers see colleagues treated badly, they leave as soon as they can. The Hay Group, a consulting firm, which conducts extensive research into the most admired companies as determined by *Fortune*'s annual survey, finds that the best ones take extra pains to reassure their "most driven and focused employees," the ones who are most important to keep, that they're valued and wanted.

Not every company will behave so wisely, which presents another opportunity: stealing outstanding performers from companies that are mistreating them. When I met with a group of HR chiefs from top-performing companies, practically all of them said they were doing this or planning to. Tempting as it is, it must be done carefully. You require sound competitive intelligence to know who the best performers really are, and it's important to determine whether they're actually being treated poorly or just like to switch jobs every time they see a slightly better deal. But assuming you've done your homework, now is a rare chance to build the most valuable capital in your business.

Pay Smart

To grab the opportunity, you must offer that wonderful human capital a pay package that will attract them without provoking mutiny among your current employees. How to pay people during a recession is a touchy subject, but the big opportunity is to get pay right, especially since it may have been twisted out of shape during the good times.

The most fundamental pay question in a recession is how to distribute the pain. No simple answer applies to everyone, and the best answer will depend heavily on a company's culture and circumstances. For example, I spoke with the HR chief of a large, successful, industrial conglomerate, who told me that all the top executives in his company were taking a pay cut of 30 percent. I asked him if he wasn't worried that competitors would swoop in to steal some of his best performers. His answer surprised me: "We're concerned about losing talent, but we figured leading from the front is a more important message to employees than losing a few key people." His company employs tens of thousands of factory workers, many of whom are being laid off, and he's right that it's valuable for them to see that the top brass are feeling some pain also. But considering the importance of superior executive talent in his industry, I'm not sure this company is making the right choice.

By contrast, sharing the pain works fine in companies with a titanium-strength culture of employee focus and lifetime employment or something close. Look at famous outfits such as Nucor Steel and Lincoln Electric. When tough times hit, they immediately eliminate all executive perks and bonuses. If that isn't enough, managers take pay cuts. If that still isn't enough, everyone works fewer days per week, with pay reduced accordingly, all in order to preserve jobs. These companies don't offer the highest pay around, yet people compete fiercely to work there because they like the culture and appreciate the security.

At the other extreme, consider Wall Street firms. A few of them possess strong employee-focused cultures, notably Goldman Sachs, but many others are about just one thing: this year's dollars. In an environment where money is the only thing that talks, employers don't have many options when they want to attract and keep good performers. For example, Morgan Stanley is buying a controlling interest in the Smith Barney brokerage firm from Citigroup, and to keep the best brokers from leaving it will pay the top performers retention bonuses amounting to millions of dollars per person in some cases. That move may seem nervy considering that Morgan Stanley has received billions in U.S. government assistance and, like all such firms, is taking heavy criticism for its pay practices. But because it's in a money-is-everything culture and keeping the best brokers is critical, the firm figures it has no choice.

The larger point is that every company can use this downturn as motivation to get its pay practices right. For example, a widespread criticism of the Wall Street firms that stumbled or fell in the financial crisis is that their pay programs encouraged too much risk; executives had much to gain if their high-risk bets paid off and little to lose if they didn't. In response, Morgan Stanley revamped its bonus system so that annual bonuses are paid out over the following three years, not in a lump sum; if an employee performs badly, some of the bonus can be canceled. It's about time that Wall Street discovered this excellent approach, which is by no means new; several industrial firms have used it for years. At Deere, for example, incentives are based on economic profit, a measure that includes capital costs, and bonuses earned in any given year are paid out over four years; again, if performance falters, part of the bonuses can be canceled. The system works well in all stages of the business cycle and is especially helpful in a recession. Deere's highly regarded CEO, Robert Lane, told me he likes it because "it encourages long-term thinking"—seeing the downturn as just one part of a larger picture—"and especially discourages doing anything that would negate earned bonuses."

Smart pay practices help stabilize a firm during hard times. Fred Smith, FedEx's founder and CEO, says, "All of our management compensation is heavily related to the performance of the company. At the first-line management level it's maybe 15 percent or 20 percent. At my level it's 90 percent. So obviously, as the economy has gotten weaker, a lot of that expense has simply gone away."

Getting pay right is never easy. Company objectives shift; methods of measuring individual performance are always imperfect; formulas for rewarding performance can almost always be gamed. Nonetheless, in a recession refining all those elements is especially valuable. Most important, are you paying for what you really want? In a downturn you may need fresh new thinking more than ever—but good luck to you if, like most companies, you're paying people mostly to avoid mistakes. Is it critical that you keep your best talent? If you're sharing the recession's pain equally—making stars accept the same sacrifices as the supporting cast—you may be in trouble.

The True Costs of Layoffs

Maybe you've tried everything and concluded that you're in one of those companies that honestly cannot avoid layoffs. Sometimes that's reality. But before you pull the trigger, consider the true costs of layoffs and whether they will actually get you the benefits you're counting on.

Layoffs are expensive in direct costs. You've noticed that when a company announces a large layoff, it records a hefty financial charge, not a revenue increase. Severance payments and other benefit costs that may be contractually required can add up to a substantial total, and most of those costs are immediate. When you consider the time value of that money, a layoff may not pay for itself for two years or even more. By that time, you could be hiring again—that is, your layoff might not actually save you any money. But even if it does, it also costs you money in several additional ways. For example:

You'll face the costs and delays of hiring and training new employees when the economy turns back up. That day will come, and when it does, companies that have held onto their workers will be able to respond far more quickly and confidently than competitors who need to find new employees and get them up to speed.

That's a lesson the oil industry learned painfully in the mid-1980s, when oil prices plunged much as they did in 2008. Companies fired tens of thousands of workers, then couldn't get enough of them back when business rebounded. Most of the major players have sworn not to repeat that mistake this time. Halliburton CEO David Lesar even told investors that while he'd have to lose some people, "our goal is to minimize the number of employees affected, to avoid the high recruitment and training costs we incur when industry fundamentals improve."

In a very different industry, Northwest Airlines learned that lesson after it fired hundreds of pilots during tough times in 2007. When business picked up later that year, it had to cancel hundreds of flights because it didn't have enough pilots. The airline scheduled its remaining pilots too aggressively, and at the end of each month many of them had used up their permissible flight hours. The company had to speed up its recall and retraining of laid-off pilots.

Valuable knowledge will walk out the door. In a knowledge-based economy, the contents of your employees' brains may be worth more than anything else in the company. Realizing this, several companies have launched projects to capture this informal and uncodified knowledge, but in general they haven't been very successful. You can't measure the knowledge that will leave with the employees you lay off, but try to imagine it. Realize that most of it will never come back.

Your company will lose productivity before, during, and after the layoff. Within ten minutes of a layoff being planned or even considered, the rumor mill will be spinning furiously. From that moment on, productivity will tank as employees trade information, prepare résumés, and spend much more time thinking about themselves than about their work. The effects will last long past the layoff itself.

Your company will damage its brand as an employer. Hundreds of companies now state an explicit goal to be an "employer of choice" in their industry or locale. That's a worthy goal in an economy where the war for talent is a long-term fact of life, even if it has been interrupted by the recession. Companies still clamor to get onto *Fortune*'s annual list of the one hundred best companies to work for more fiercely every year. How badly will a layoff damage your company's ability to attract the best talent?

Top law firms compete ferociously for the best new lawyers, yet many of those firms are laying people off. New York–based Simpson Thacher & Bartlett figured this was the moment to offer associates a chance to take a year off to work on a public service project and get paid $60,000 plus benefits—less than half their normal pay but a lot better than nothing. And it makes the firm much more attractive to the next crop of law school graduates.

Southwest Airlines CEO Gary Kelly understands the point. The company has had no layoffs in its thirty-eight years, and while he makes no promises about the future, he knows what's at stake. "It's one thing to say it, but you have to prove to your people that you really do love them and care about them," he says. "And if you have layoffs every five years, or if you make a promise to your employees that you don't fulfill, and you do that often, well, it's kind of hard to hold out that your employees are really the most valued part of the company."

Your leadership pipeline will suffer years from now. Layoffs greatly increase the chances that you're firing a future company leader. You may never know who, but the effect is real. The banking industry and the electric utility industry both went through severe cutbacks in the 1980s, and executives in both industries have told me that they paid a heavy price twenty years later—when they needed experienced, knowledgeable leaders to succeed the generation that was retiring and found only a broad empty space in the ranks.

Even the survivors will pay a price. Wally Bock, an independent consultant on leadership, says survivors "will certainly experience some grief. They may also still fear the loss of their own job." Sometimes the effects are much worse. Workers who remain after a layoff make considerably more medical claims, especially for mental health, substance abuse, and cardiovascular issues, reports a study by Cigna and the American Management Association. Research from the Beth Israel Deaconess Medical Center in Boston found that managers are twice as likely to suffer a heart attack in the week after they fire someone.

Wall Street's reaction may be the opposite of what you expect. Don't count on a layoff announcement to make your stock go up. It might, if you're laying off people because you're combining two companies in a merger, according to research from Bain & Company. But if you're laying off employees as a cost-cutting measure, Wall Street will likely see it as a sign of major trouble—and send your stock down.

Put all those factors together and you realize why layoffs should be very nearly a company's last option in responding to a recession. Still, sometimes the last option is all you've got left. So let's assume that despite all the dangers, you absolutely must make a layoff. Even in this last-resort situation, you can find a couple of opportunities.

First is the opportunity to lose some people you should have lost long ago. If you're laying off twenty thousand unionized factory workers, you can't do this. But if you're able to choose the individuals who will go, this is a chance to atone for years of managerial sins. Most companies are terrible at rigorous talent management. Often they have a culture in which candid assessments aren't acceptable. Everyone is told they're doing fine, even when that's a lie. Changing such a culture during good times can be virtually impossible; Jacques Nasser tried it when he was CEO of Ford Motor Company in the 1990s and lost his job. But in a truly dire recession, that culture can be changed at last.

Remember: everyone in the company knows who the weakest performers are. Management's failure to get rid of them has been sapping morale and dragging the company down for years. Now is the time to get right with that issue—and then stay right.

The second opportunity in a layoff is to send a message to the remaining employees and to the world. First you have to make the case that layoffs are truly unavoidable. Then you want to show that your company always treats its people well, even in the worst circumstances. You needn't be a giant company to do it. Zappos, the online shoe retailer that's on *Fortune*'s list of the best companies to work for, had to lay off 124 employees in 2008. The company gave them generous severance pay, six months of free medical coverage after they left, and continuation of their 40 percent employee discount through Christmas, though none of that was required.

Survivors will still be nervous, but such generosity makes a difference. "How you treat the leavers has a strong impact on how the stayers feel about the company," says Beth Axelrod, HR chief at eBay, which also treated its recently laid off employees with considerable humanity.

The message a company sends through its people practices is just one part of a larger issue facing every company today. This recession, more than any since the Depression, is deeply changing the relationships between business and the rest of the world—employees, customers, suppliers, investors, government. Understanding such a profound change and adapting to it is another skill that most business leaders haven't had to learn. Now they must. We turn to it next.

CHAPTER FIVE

Engage the Outside World

All your relationships are changing—so take control of the process

You know you're in trouble when the late-night TV comedians turn against you—which means that if the world's bankers remained in any doubt about their public standing as of 2009, they could easily get a reading on it. For example:

> Well, today the heads of the eight largest banks testified before Congress. Bank CEOs in a room full of politicians—they had to flip a coin to see who's going to tell the first lie. *—Jay Leno*

Sometimes the joke's victims are much more specific:

> And Citigroup, who received a huge bailout from the government, owns the naming rights to the New York Mets' new stadium. It is currently called Citi Field, but because of Barack Obama's crackdown on the federal bailout money, Citigroup will legally have to change the name of the stadium to Money Grubbing Bastards Field. *—Jay Leno*

These jokes, and many, many others like them, fall into a category of humor that actually isn't screamingly funny—but audiences love it because it dares to express the rage they feel. That rage is part of a culturally huge phenomenon that circles the globe, a major shift in the relationships between business and the larger society. It affects every category of relationship—with the general public, employees, customers, investors, government—and it is, appropriately, the largest such shift since the Depression. At a time like this it's easy for business leaders to feel under siege. But the best ones understand that such a large change in the world is full of new opportunities.

To make the most of those opportunities, it's necessary first to accept the magnitude of the change and the considerable length of time the effects will likely last. Human nature pushes us to minimize it, to imagine that things will continue pretty much as they were, just altered around the edges. But this is a change in the very atmosphere that companies breathe. To appreciate that, remember how fundamentally business's world changed during the Depression. Governments built vast new regulatory structures to oversee business that are still with us, such as the Securities and Exchange Commission in the United States; the attendant laws and regulations have been multiplying for seventy-five years. More broadly, government's role in the economy mushroomed—permanently, it seems. Government spending was 9 percent of U.S. GDP in 1929; by 1940 it was 15 percent, and since then the proportion has never gone lower.

Union membership rocketed during the Depression and then continued rising. At the same time, a new view of the relationship between management and employees took hold. Frederick Taylor, the time-and-motion specialist who regarded people as programmable machines with an unfortunate tendency to think for themselves, had dominated managerial thinking until then; Henry Ford famously complained that he had to hire a whole person when all he wanted was a pair of hands. But the suffering of the Depression drove home an idea being advanced by psychologist Elton Mayo and humanist writer Mary Parker Follett—that treating workers like human beings was smarter.

Today's crisis is no Depression, but it too will change business's world for decades. Finding opportunity in that shift may seem tough when public attitudes appear to be moving massively against business. But remember, your company isn't business—it's one company. As an analogy, it has been shown many times that most people don't like Congress but do like their own congressman. You needn't suffer from a growing antibusiness animus if you can first resist the temptation to underestimate it, then get ahead of it and focus on distinguishing yourself from the pack. Indeed, there's no better time to look good than when the competition is despised.

Yes, You Can Still Be Admired

The plunge in the public's regard for business is evident worldwide. Across twenty countries, 62 percent of survey respondents said in late 2008 that they trusted business less than they had a year earlier, according to the Trust Barometer published annually by the Edelman public relations firm. The decline is worst in the United States, where 77 percent said they trusted business less. This is how bad it is: trust in U.S. business is even lower than it was after Enron and the dotcom bust.

The trend appeared similar, though not quite as bad, in Western Europe, but then Europe fell into recession a bit later than the United States did. If the survey were conducted again, with unemployment rising and home values falling across Europe, it might well show that attitudes there had caught up with U.S. levels of distrust.

This all matters because the way consumers regard companies affects the products they will buy, the stocks they will invest in, and the public policies they will support. In the United States, the two industries suffering the deepest declines in trust are the two industries being bailed out by government: banks and autos. The drops are vertiginous: trust in banks fell from 69 percent to 36 percent in one year, and in auto companies from 60 percent to 33 percent.

Understanding that trend is important, but even more important is understanding the exceptions: not every company—not even every company in those miserable industries—is scorned. Some companies are still truly admired. *Fortune*'s 2009 ranking of the world's most admired companies, determined by a global survey of businesspeople, identified companies that in today's environment look better than ever. The top five: Apple, Berkshire Hathaway, Toyota, Google, Johnson & Johnson. Note that number three, Toyota, is a most admired company in a most reviled industry. In addition, the top twenty firms in the ranking include three banks: Wells Fargo, JPMorgan Chase, and Goldman Sachs. As firms that stayed strong while many about them were crumbling, they look better today than they did when times were good.

A deeper analysis of the most admired companies was conducted by the Hay Group, a management consulting firm, which has been studying this ranking for years. The central question: what traits do these top companies share? Most important, Hay found, is a strong, stable strategy, which confers important benefits in unstable times. Companies that change strategies must usually change organizational structures as well, and making that change in a recession is a heavy burden just when companies can bear it least. It forces employees to focus inward rather than outward and becomes a giant sink of time and energy.

By contrast, companies whose strategies hold up in a recession can press ahead undistracted and make major competitive gains. Southwest Airlines, which has ranked high on this list for the past thirteen years, hasn't changed its strategy because of the recession—in fact, hasn't changed it in thirty-eight years, as CEO Gary Kelly notes: "To this day we still operate one aircraft type [the Boeing 737]. We still fly in the domestic U.S. We still operate with a single class of service. We just try to be really good at what we do."

Hay found that in general, less admired companies change structures far more often than the most admired, the main reason being a strategy switch. An extreme example is the Detroit automakers, which are turning themselves inside out seeking strategies for survival at a moment when they should be focused on serving buyers. By contrast, the most admired "are more confident in their strategies and, as a result, are more likely to use this opportunity for rapid expansion and a chance to take market share," says Mel Stark, who oversees Hay's research on these firms. He found that they're far likelier to be expanding globally now than are their less admired peers.

A good example is Coca-Cola. CEO Muhtar Kent says, "One thing we don't do in this crisis is cut marketing around the world. We continue to make sure that our brands stay healthy and that we exit this tunnel with more market share than when we went in." For strong companies, now is an especially good time to do that: "Crises offer you the best opportunity to communicate with consumers because airwaves are cleaner—there's much less congestion on the airwaves."

It's thus clear that public regard is part of a virtuous circle that's especially powerful in a deep recession. Admiration and financial success feed each other, and in tough times economic strength helps a company look even better than competitors—and also enables it to shape its message to the public.

Help Shape the Narrative

Shaping not just a company's own message but also business's message in general is critical now because we're at a turning point. Something economically giant has taken place, and ordinary people worldwide are struggling to answer the basic question: what happened? The answer on which they settle will powerfully influence laws, the culture, and individual behavior. Several possible answers are contending for dominance, so if you care about which answer wins, now is the time to speak up.

The publicly embraced answer will be short, simple, and not entirely correct—a stereotype, as the journalist Walter Lippmann first used the term. Historic events are complicated, and the public always settles on explanations that simplify. Speculation caused the 1929 market crash, Hoover turned it into the Great Depression, FDR got us out of it—no historian would fully endorse any of those statements, but they're what most people think, and what people think is what politicians, media, business, and the society respond to.

As for what caused this financial crisis and recession, the short, simple, flawed, accepted answer is likely to be one of these four:

Free markets ran amok. The broad deregulatory trend of the past thirty years finally went too far. MIT-trained geniuses cooked up new ways to buy, slice, dice, reconstitute, and sell mortgages as novel securities that no one really understood but that investors were willing to buy because rating agencies—clueless, conflicted, and unregulated—said they were solid. Mortgage brokers were permitted to confuse and deceive prospects. Supposedly undergirding the whole system was a multitrillion-dollar market in credit default swaps that was totally unregulated. When government fails to police the financial sector strictly, this is what happens.

Greenspan did it. In the late 1990s, when he well knew that stock prices were irrational, he failed to put the brakes on; and then, trying to rescue the economy after the resulting market bust from 2000 to 2002, he cut interest rates too far too fast. Credit became insanely easy to get throughout the economy, and everybody but him could see it. He even reassured the United States that there wasn't any housing bubble, such words from the maestro emboldening hapless home buyers to continue down their doomed path of paying and borrowing ever more money. When one person gains so much influence over the financial system and screws up, the result is disaster.

Clinton and the Democrat-controlled Congress twisted the system. To gain favor with the lower-income voters who are an important part of their base, they heavily revised the Community Reinvestment Act in 1995 and took other measures that virtually forced lenders to give mortgages to subprime borrowers. Remember the outcry over redlining, the practice of refusing to lend for home buying in certain neighborhoods? Congress sure fixed that, and now those neighborhoods are the hot zones of the foreclosure crisis. Banks that refused to lend to those borrowers weren't evil, they were prudent—until Clinton and Congress made that illegal.

Americans, Britons, Spaniards, Australians, and many other consumers worldwide lost their self-discipline. Everybody forgot that financial life requires hard work and is filled with risk. In the old days, mortgage lenders had good reasons for demanding that borrowers submit mountains of paperwork and make a 20 percent down payment, and borrowers quite rightly felt their hearts in their throats when they signed the note. All of that disappeared from 2002 to 2007. Millions of people in every part of the system chose to believe that they could get rich quickly, easily, and safely, that work and risk assessment no longer mattered. When whole societies decide to abandon basic virtues, large-scale trouble is certain.

It's fine to argue that the real answer is a nuanced combination of all these and many other factors, but that won't do. Public opinion will settle on an explanation of one sentence, maybe two, and it's obvious how differing explanations imply deeply different policy responses and different directions for the culture.

As for what actually happened, of course I like the nuanced combination of factors. But if forced to order off the menu above, I'd say that answer number four is the most nearly correct. Nonetheless, I suspect that answer number one will prevail, with far-reaching consequences—especially for government policy.

Indeed, research suggests this is already happening. Around the world, people believe by overwhelming margins that "government should intervene to regulate industry or nationalize companies to restore public trust," according to Edelman's Trust Barometer. In the United States not even half (49 percent) say that "the free market should be allowed to function independently." Now governments everywhere are giving their constituents what they want.

The New Relationship with Government

Barney Frank, the Massachusetts congressman who chairs the powerful House Financial Services Committee—and is thus one of the most important people influencing business anywhere—said in late 2008 that he believed 2009 would be "the best year for public policy since the Great Depression." Not many businesspeople shared his enthusiasm.

A good year for Frank is one with lots and lots of new business regulation, and he was surely right in expecting a record harvest, not just in the United States but worldwide. In the long run, the news-dominating nationalization of various banks and bailouts of automakers may prove a less significant aspect of government's growing role; though drastic, those measures are temporary. More worthy of concern for most businesspeople are the new rules, structures, and policies being developed by governments globally, which will shape business behavior for decades.

Only a few companies are big enough to influence government during this critical period. The challenge for most of us will be understanding what's coming, then thinking deeply about what it will mean for our businesses and adapting to the new reality before our competitors.

Change is on the way in four broad categories:

New regulation of leverage, risk, and risk markets. A major element of the emerging conventional view of the recession is that out-of-control risk was a prime cause. It was indeed, though it wasn't all the type of risk that government should or could have squelched.

Much of it was simply a mania, investors willfully ignoring risk in the heady, doomed belief that it had somehow disappeared, as noted in chapter 1; when people are intent on behaving that way, it's tough to rescue them from themselves. Yet such thinking smacks of defeatism in today's environment. Risk is a dirty word, and government means to blunt its potential dangers.

The methods will likely include restricting leverage in financial institutions, and certainly some of the failed investment banks were crazily overleveraged, with each dollar of equity supporting thirty-five or forty dollars of debt. Some of the remaining investment banks, having voluntarily converted themselves into commercial banks, already face capital requirements, and these could be made more stringent. Government could also impose much more nebulous antirisk measures. When the U.S. government gave TARP money to banks, it required that incentive pay at the affected firms not "encourage unnecessary and excessive risks that threaten the value of the financial institution." What that really means is entirely a matter of judgment, but the message is clear: play it safe, or Washington could land on you hard. Similar requirements could end up in regulations affecting other financial institutions.

Risk taking could be restricted in other ways. The world's largest insurer, AIG, got into trouble mainly through heavy bets on credit default swaps, a form of bond insurance. Use of such instruments will likely be regulated, as will trading in them, which had been conducted privately rather than through established exchanges.

The big picture shows government crimping risk taking by established financial players. That shift poses major questions for most companies: where will you get your capital, and how much will it cost? Advancing capital always involves risk; will the banks or other institutions you may have depended on still be willing and able to supply it? Will they charge more for it? What about insurance—will new restrictions on risk taking raise its cost, or even prevent you from getting it?

Large-scale new regulatory frameworks. Another key element of the emerging narrative of the recession is that it represents a broad regulatory failure, so broad that merely imposing new rules may not be enough. Government agencies created over decades in response to differing needs could be combined or redirected. In the United States, for example, Congress created the SEC during the Depression and the Public Company Accounting Oversight Board after the Enron and WorldCom scandals; several agencies oversee banks. The story is similar in most other developed economies. Some of these entities will certainly be combined into new ones, creating new challenges for companies that have spent years getting to know their regulators. Now every company must ask: What government agencies will be regulating us a year from now? Pursuing what mission? Directed and staffed by whom?

Protectionism and other employment programs. They started as soon as the recession did and have taken many forms. "Buy local" requirements are in stimulus packages worldwide. The European Union imposed duties on steel rods imported from China and Moldova after a thousand steelworkers demonstrated in Brussels. French president Nicolas Sarkozy publicly chastised French automakers for continuing to manufacture cars outside France—with an implicit threat of government action if the companies didn't shape up—and governments across Europe are offering consumers thousands of euros to replace their old cars with new ones. The United States announced plans to lend airlines billions of dollars for buying Boeing airplanes, and France said it would lend billions for buying Airbus planes; Brazil had to respond and said it would offer loans for buying planes from Embraer.

Such moves directly contradict the promises of global cooperation that all these nations make regularly at meetings of the G-7, G-8, and G-20, which shows (in case anyone wondered) that domestic political needs always trump pledges to other countries. All this despite universal agreement that protectionism was a principal factor in turning the economic downturn of the early 1930s into the Great Depression.

Every company needs to understand how it will be affected by these moves—and the effects touch almost every firm. It isn't just a matter of whether your exports will be blocked by foreign protection or your domestic sales increased by your own country's initiatives. Second- and third-order effects can be at least as important. For example, who will supply the engines and other components for those Boeing and Airbus planes? The U.S. stimulus program provides billions of dollars to support domestic automakers—but also billions for mass transit, which would reduce demand for cars. Stimulus programs worldwide include lots of spending on infrastructure, partly because bridges and roads are a highly local business with few foreign players—but even if you're not in the asphalt business, how will the new infrastructure affect the localities where you operate? On balance, will global protection and employment programs help you or your competitors more?

Greater government activism in areas less directly connected to resolving the crisis. As governments fly to the rescue of the global economy, they quickly get used to their larger role and gain confidence to do even more. We see the effects first in industries being bailed out. In the United States, for example, Congress at the last minute added a provision to its stimulus bill that would directly—and clumsily—regulate executive pay at banks receiving government help. No one, not even supporters of the provision, argued that it would help the banks perform better or get free of government assistance sooner; it only punished executives (many of whom had no role in the banks' problems) and allowed legislators to issue press releases.

Similarly, Congressman Frank publicly criticized Citigroup for its naming-rights deal with the Mets that Jay Leno made fun of, and Frank tried to force the bank to break the deal, but the contract was binding. Frank is an expert on many things but most assuredly not on marketing—yet he presumed to dictate how a for-profit business could and couldn't market itself. Nor was he deterred by his inability to bust up Citi's deal with the Mets. "We can't force them to break an existing contract," he told the *New York Times*, "but we can put in some pretty strict conditions on them going forward."

It's reasonable to expect this trend to spread into areas such as environmental regulation, business-labor relations, antitrust enforcement, and others, all of which can be related to the recession, if only tenuously, in one way or another. The challenge for companies will be imagining all that might happen and how it would affect them. In this, as in so much else, the bigger and bolder thinkers will probably be better prepared.

Get Right with the Street

That law restricting executive pay at banks included an additional requirement: any bank receiving TARP assistance must allow shareholders an annual vote on whether they approve or disapprove of the firm's executive pay in general. These "say on pay" votes had been making slow progress through corporations, with a few adopting them and most others violently resisting them. But now the whole relationship between companies and owners is changing dramatically, and not just because of legislation.

One day in February 2009, Unilever startled investors worldwide by announcing that it really didn't know what its profit for the year would be. As for a previously announced goal of increasing profits 15 percent in 2010—well, it had no idea if that would happen either. Paul Polman, the new CEO, explained, "This is an exceptional time. . . . We live in a time of ambiguity."

He's right, and this exceptional time is an excellent opportunity for other companies to free themselves from the useless habit of publicly predicting their own earnings, otherwise known as giving guidance. The guidance game has developed gradually over decades, so those in its midst may have trouble seeing how insane it has become. But consider the typical scenario, which has been repeated literally thousands of times. A company begins the new quarter by encouraging analysts to forecast strong earnings growth. Then, as the weeks pass, the company tries to talk that forecast down by issuing careful press releases. When the consensus is low enough, the company announces it is "comfortable" with Wall Street's view. The quarter ends, and the company announces—what do you know?—that it has beaten the estimate. The stock is supposed to rise on this positive "surprise," but investors caught on and realized the consensus estimate might be bogus. They wanted the real earnings forecast, and the infamous "whisper number" was born. If a company doesn't beat it, its stock can fall even if it surpasses the published earnings consensus. So companies have had to start guiding the whisper number also.

Of course, this game produces nothing good and can lead to much harm as managers feel pressured to hit the announced target at all costs. The trouble is that many CEOs truly believe they can't stop playing. As with trade loading or heroin abuse, quitting suddenly would be fatal, they think. Fortunately, it just isn't so, as many companies have shown. GlaxoSmithKline also ended guidance in 2009, just as Barry Diller did with his companies in the 2001 recession. The world didn't end, and their stocks went up. While suddenly ceasing guidance in good times may alarm investors, they understand that in a historic recession even the best companies can't predict results a year down the road. That's why this is such a promising time for a company to recast its relationship with investors and drop out of the guidance game.

This opportunity for companies to free themselves from an onerous, self-imposed obligation is being more than offset by new obligations, imposed by others, that will affect companies' relationships with investors. The say-on-pay requirement in the U.S. stimulus bill is no surprise; during the election campaign, both Obama and his opponent, John McCain, said they favored a law requiring all publicly traded companies to offer shareholders such a vote. We can expect further new requirements also giving shareholders more power—imposed not by governments but by the shareholders themselves.

Trends in this direction have been developing for several years, but as long as stock markets were rising, many investors just didn't pay much attention. Now, as stock prices have dropped to levels not seen in more than a decade, shareholders have grown intensely interested in governance and are strongly positioned to make sudden gains. Companies will want to assess how they'd be affected by newly powerful shareholder demands for change in three areas:

Majority voting for directors. In most companies, board directors have always been chosen through Soviet-style elections. For each position there is exactly one candidate; please mark your choice. If you don't like a candidate you can withhold your vote, but as long as he gets at least one vote—which he can cast for himself, assuming he owns at least one share—then he is elected. Shareholders have long insisted that only directors who get a majority of votes cast have any claim to legitimacy. Now a growing number of companies—impelled by shareholder resolutions—are changing their rules to require majority votes for directors.

Shareholder access to the proxy. If majority voting sounds radical—which, incredibly, it does at many companies—how about this: letting shareholders nominate director candidates to run against the board's own nominees. Most companies hate this idea, but it may have legs. Two judges of the Delaware Court of Chancery, arguably the world's most important corporate legal venue—Delaware being the state where most large U.S. companies are incorporated—have addressed this issue very sympathetically: "If this philosophy [of independent directors] is so central to our system of corporate governance, one can rightly ask why the current incumbent-biased corporate election process should be perpetuated," they wrote. If a case on this matter gets to court, these two men will be judging it. And when people question whether something should be "perpetuated," it means they think it shouldn't be.

Shareholder voting procedures. This issue is low on sex appeal but high in importance. Shareholders must vote on directors as well as various resolutions, but the voting isn't like political voting. It takes place over a period of days or weeks, and during that time managers can monitor the results—but shareholders can't. Ballots are not secret. If managers don't like the way a vote is going, they can lobby major shareholders to change their votes, which is perfectly legal. For example, when Carly Fiorina was CEO of Hewlett-Packard and was campaigning furiously for shareholder approval of her proposed merger with Compaq, she crisscrossed America meeting with major shareholders while voting was taking place; that merger eventually won approval with 51.4 percent of the vote. In political elections, questions of which ballots are valid get decided with representatives of all parties in the room—but in corporate elections, shareholders aren't present. As shareholder democracy gets pushed forward on other fronts, watch for reform of fundamental voting procedures.

This downturn is reordering the relationship between companies and shareholders, so every company will need to form a position on these issues and decide how to respond. For example, majority voting has taken hold in the United States, and many companies, such as Dell, FedEx, and Intel, have adopted it voluntarily. On other fronts, a company may wish to fight. The key is realizing that the atmosphere is changing, and positions that made sense in 2007 might not be wise today.

In all of a company's relationships with the larger world, communicating much more than usual is a big help in tough times. Everyone you interact with is worried or uncertain—shareholders are anxious about your strategy or maybe your cash position, regulators wonder what unexpected problems you may throw at them, communities fear you might close down operations. If these constituencies don't hear from you, they just worry more, and that makes relationships more awkward and less productive. Communicating with them may seem like an obvious response, but in fact it's the opposite of most people's instincts. We all tend to keep quiet when we don't have answers—to "hunker in the bunker," as American Express CEO Ken Chenault expressed it to me, until we feel we have something definite to say. That's exactly the wrong approach. A company's constituencies don't expect you to have all the answers. They just want to hear your view of the world, to understand how you're approaching your situation, and to know that you're thinking about them. In bad times they need to hear all this much, much more than when times are good.

Just as your relations with outside constituencies are being reordered in this recession, all the relationships you have in your industry—with customers, suppliers, competitors—are shifting as well, maybe dramatically. For that reason, your strategy and business model need reexamining with a fresh eye. That's our next topic.

CHAPTER SIX

Reexamine Your Strategy and Business Model

The importance of knowing what you must change—and what you must not

On a freezing night in February 2009, Giorgio Armani stood in the center of his brand-new store on Fifth Avenue in Manhattan, the host of the store's glittering, celebrity-filled grand opening. The U.S. recession was in its fourteenth month. In New York, tens of thousands of former investment bankers were out of work, their magnificent year-end bonuses cut drastically or completely, their prospects unattractive. Much of the New York City economy, and a huge portion of the luxury goods industry in which Armani operates, depends on these now unemployed people and their multimillion-dollar incomes.

Yet Armani pushed ahead with the opening of his store, a space that would have seemed stunning even in the headiest economic boom. Calling it a shop would not be accurate. Standing at the corner of Fifty-sixth Street, one of the most expensive retail locations on earth, it occupies forty-three thousand square feet devoted to three separate merchandise collections, a restaurant, and a chocolate shop. Armani wasn't saying what it had cost, but a good guess would be something close to $40 million—to open the most extravagant store in New York in the depths of the worst recession in seventy-five years.

The obvious question: was he crazy? Time will tell, but he seemed serenely confident in what he had done. "An entrepreneur shows his true colors in a period of crisis, not in a period when everybody is having success," he was quoted as saying. He seemed to understand the financial reality of it all: "Understand that the investments that I made in this store I will probably not get back for twenty to twenty-five years," he said, displaying a long-term orientation that most of us can only admire—especially considering that he was seventy-four years old when he said it.

Three Questions

Would you have the courage to invest a ton of money in an audacious project during a terrible recession? You would if you were utterly certain of your business's core, of its central, unchangeable meaning. Armani understood that recession or no, certain traits of his company would not waver: the design sensibility established over forty years, its standing as a preeminent luxury brand, its assertive yet tasteful way of engaging retail customers. The new Manhattan store embodied all those things. He would cut costs elsewhere if necessary, but not there.

Armani's decision to go ahead with his New York store raises a larger issue that all companies face in a bad recession. Is our strategy going to work in this environment? What must we change—and what must we not change? Will the recession fundamentally change our industry and our place in it? Or will this downturn just throw us off the long-term trend line for a couple of years? Do we need a new business model?

Those are large and deep questions for any company, and reconsidering strategy can turn into a miasma that consumes endless time and yields nothing. Yet the process is manageable. One way to think through the matter of your strategy and business model in this recession is to answer three basic questions.

1. What is our core?

A finding that's consistent across many recessions is that the best-performing companies keep investing in their core, no matter how bad things get. One of the most inspiring examples is what DuPont decided about research during the Depression. As revenues plunged in that downturn's first three years, the company reduced its R & D spending commensurately. But then the company's leaders realized that this policy would destroy the firm's future. Leading-edge research and the resulting new products were the very heart of the company. Elmer Bolton, who became famous as DuPont's director of chemical research, wrote that "it is a demonstrated fact that progress in the expansion of an industry cannot be accomplished by intermittent efforts in research that is curtailed at the first sign of reduced profits." So DuPont resolved to keep funding chemical research—its core—straight through the Depression, no matter what. Among the results: nylon, neoprene, and other products that brought DuPont billions of dollars over the following decades.

Excellent companies are certain of their core. Early in this recession, Brad Smith, CEO of the Intuit software firm, told us at *Fortune*, "We're not going to cut innovation. This company for twenty-five years has been fueled by new product innovation. We're protecting the innovation pipeline so we come out of this strong." He would cut elsewhere if necessary, but in the realm of personal and small-business finance software, he's up against mammoth competitors, including Microsoft. He cannot afford to fall even a fraction of a generation behind them.

As wonderful as innovation is, it isn't every company's core. Kohl's, the big midmarket retailer, spent more on marketing in the recessionary 2008 holiday season than it had in 2007 because marketing is part of its core. Like Intuit, it's also threatened by a giant—in this case Wal-Mart—and can't give up even an inch of territory, regardless of tough times. At Domino's Pizza, a key element of the core is delivering the pizza within thirty minutes. No matter how the company chooses to cope with this recession, it will not jeopardize the delivery time. Several market trends favor pizza just now—it's a low-cost food that's consumed at home—but Chris Moore, CEO of Domino's in the UK, told a British magazine that "none of that means anything to us unless we can deliver the pizza on time." He understands his company's core.

For some companies, investing in the core is mandatory for maintaining the firm's competitive position. For other companies it can be a powerful way to extend the firm's lead and pound competitors that are already suffering. An instructive example is Intel, which announced plans to invest $7 billion to upgrade technology at its plants in 2009 and 2010. Intel has a high cost of capital, so such a large investment would be brave in any environment, but consider that the firm was announcing it at the beginning of a year when overall microchip demand was forecast to drop by 25 to 30 percent. Most of its competitors were cutting way back on capacity, and its most direct competitor, Advanced Micro Devices, was spinning off its manufacturing operations entirely. Yet Intel was choosing this moment to strengthen its core. Foreseeing how advantageously it will be positioned when the economy rebounds was not difficult.

For many companies, investing in the core requires first deciding what the core is. That's a valuable discussion to have at any time, and especially in a recession; what it often reveals is that the concept of the core was forgotten during the good times. That's when companies wander into businesses for which they command no special capability but that get along while the economy is strong. Then, when the downturn hits, the noncore businesses blow up and have to be axed. It has happened this time just as it always does. Pioneer, the Japanese maker of audio and other electronic products, bailed out of the grindingly competitive flat-screen TV business. Home Depot shut down its Expo chain of home design centers. UBS closed businesses that dealt in real estate and U.S. municipal bonds. Even Google, while still highly profitable, closed down noncore businesses that sold advertising on radio stations and in newspapers. None of those companies could keep investing in the core as long as money-losing noncore businesses continued to drain cash.

Of course, it's possible for the core to change, especially in momentous times like these. Entire industries can be restructured, and wise companies may have to shift their core in response. A bit later we'll consider the issue of whether this recession is altering your business so significantly that you need to rethink your core. But if that isn't happening, then the exercise of understanding your true core, and gaining the confidence to invest in it even now, will create strengths that will last a long time. Consider Procter & Gamble, which understands that product innovation and brand building are at the center of all it does. It's investing in gene-based research to create better cosmetics. When the decoding of the human genome was hailed as one of the great scientific achievements of all time, you probably weren't thinking about how it could lead to wrinkle-smoothing skin cream, but P&G scientists were. It turns out there's also a genomic angle to dandruff and the gum disease gingivitis. No one knows if the company's research will produce any breakthrough products, but it certainly could, and if even one or two prove successful, P&G's competitive advantage—and the financial benefits—could be vast.

That's the power of knowing your core and having the confidence to keep investing in it. But even if you're clear about that, your world is still shifting, and you must ask the next question.

2. How is this recession changing our customers and their behavior?

In chapter 8 we'll look at how successful companies adjust their value propositions to meet the changing needs of specific customers. But from a strategic perspective, we need to consider the larger question of how the recession is creating broad shifts in customers and what they want. Spotting those shifts and responding to them before competitors do is a valuable way to avoid new threats and make hay from new opportunities.

A recession as wide and deep as this one can change behavior in significant ways. In the Depression, when the U.S. unemployment rate reached 25 percent, people became devoted to radio listening like never before or since. Social workers found that Americans who needed to raise money to pay the rent would sell their refrigerators, bathtubs, telephones, and beds before they would part with their radios. The effects of Depression-induced radio mania were transformative for radio set manufacturers, radio station owners, radio performers, advertisers, ad agencies, and many other businesses.

We're all familiar with the Depression generation's ultracautious attitudes toward investing and jobs. Such attitudes were hardly surprising, and this recession could affect today's young people similarly, with long-lasting consequences for financial services firms and others. Companies began responding almost immediately, with several marketing "ultrasafe" investment vehicles, often with considerable fees attached. Traumatized investors are willing to pay more for safety than they have been in a long time.

Some other effects of bad times are more surprising. For example, in developed economies physical health tends to improve during a downturn. Exactly why isn't clear, though maybe it's because people eat healthier food, drink less, possibly smoke less, and drive less. From whatever cause, researchers have found that in the United States, a 1 percent increase in the unemployment rate correlates with a 0.5 percent decline in the death rate, and similar results have turned up in Australia and other advanced countries.

How will the recession affect your customers? Sometimes the consequences seem obvious, yet some companies fail to foresee them. In the personal computer business, it doesn't take a genius to figure that consumers will probably move toward less expensive machines. That trend would clearly seem to favor netbooks, also called mini-notebooks—smaller devices with fewer features and lower prices. Yet self-evident as all that may seem, many of the world's top PC makers, such as Dell and Hewlett-Packard, were late to the party, while makers such as Acer and ASUSTeK Computer were cashing in on the new demand for those machines. Acer's CEO, J. T. Wang, was frankly surprised: "We found out that our American competitors are not aggressive in [the netbook] segment," he was quoted as saying, "but we think this segment is very big." It's big and growing fast because of the recession.

In other ways the recession's effects on customers are not obvious. While consumers spend less overall, for example, they don't spend less on everything; they actually spend much more on certain things, and the changes in consumption patterns aren't necessarily what you might expect. During the previous two recessions (1990–91 and 2001), U.S. consumers cut sharply their spending on food away from home—no surprise there. But they also cut their consumption of tobacco products, despite the addictive nature of those items. Consumers spent less on leisure, broadly defined, though conventional wisdom holds that people spend more on entertainment to cheer themselves up when times are tough.

The spectrum's other end includes several surprises. Consumers considerably increased their spending on health care, for example. That result may be specific to the United States, where some 60 percent of health-care spending is funneled through employer-sponsored coverage; employees, worried about losing their jobs, increase their doctor visits and try to address every possible health issue while they're still employed and still covered. Consumers also spent more on personal insurance and pensions, which may seem odd at a time when we'd expect people to be focused on their most immediate needs. Again, the prospect of losing their jobs—or the actual loss of them—combined with a newly sharpened consciousness of the risks they face, probably explains the trend. The category of spending that increased most (among those studied by McKinsey, which compiled this information) was education. This also may seem surprising, considering that it too is a discretionary purchase that yields its benefits years in the future. Why spend more on something like that when every bit of income is increasingly precious? The answer seems to be that many people figured they may as well improve their employability at a time when they can't get a decent job or perhaps any job. As for the cost, they can probably borrow some or all of it and pay it back when they get a new and better job. The trend seems to be playing out in this recession as well. Applications to U.S. business schools rose markedly as the economy deteriorated.

The larger point is that as the recession alters buyer behavior, the effects may be counterintuitive and need to be addressed fast. They may not require changes in business strategy, but they may well demand adjustments to the business model, with resources shifted to the new opportunities—taking advantage of the fact that in a recession, some businesses actually grow.

A deep global recession changes much more than buyer behavior, of course. It alters the courses of national economies, reshapes capital markets, strengthens or weakens suppliers—all of which can reorder whole industries. Which leads to the next question.

3. Will this recession hasten—or even cause—a large-scale restructuring of our industry, and if so, how will it affect us?

Extreme economic conditions have a way of accelerating trends that were already under way. Excellent examples in this recession involve the media industry and U.S. automakers. In the media world, newspapers have been in decline for many years as the Internet has lured away readers with free content and has siphoned off highly profitable classified advertising. Those trends have been apparent since 1995, clearly dooming many newspapers, yet these papers hung on until the current recession, which finally pushed them over the edge. The story in autos is remarkably similar, with the secular decline of the three Detroit manufacturers observable for at least twenty years. Those companies limped from year to year, progressing with excruciating slowness toward a clearly inevitable future as much smaller outfits, possibly merging with outside firms or with one another. This recession just compressed the timeline from years to months.

The pattern is similar, if not necessarily so apocalyptic, in most big, old, product-based industries. Production has been shifting from higher-cost facilities in the developed world to lower-cost facilities in the developing world, and this recession has hastened that trend. Look for it to happen in the chemical industry, for example. In newer industries, by contrast, even a recession as bad as this one may just throw production temporarily off its long-term trend line. The growth of information technology, for example, has lurched through peaks and valleys but over time has followed a reliably rising line. A few years of below-trend growth will most likely be followed by a catch-up period of above-average growth.

Knowing which kind of future your industry faces—a world-changing, once-in-a-lifetime revolution or an era of major adaptation—is critical before you can form your response. A danger in a recession as deep as this one is that it may accelerate trends that will affect your business but that weren't even on your worry list. Three broad, multi-industry trends, already well under way, are especially worth watching because a bad recession could fuel them significantly.

Cocreation. The idea is that the most successful companies no longer invent new products and services on their own. They create them along with their customers, and they do it in a way that produces a unique experience for each customer. The critically important corollary is that no company owns enough resources, or can possibly own enough, to furnish unique experiences for every customer, so companies must organize a constantly shifting global web of suppliers and partners to do the job. In good times, the incentives to rethink a business in such bold terms are weak. But in a historic recession, a substantially different business model that may demand far fewer resources is a suddenly attractive proposition. The starkest examples so far involve the Internet. Facebook isn't a product or a service, but rather a platform on which users create their own unique experiences; since it opened itself to software applications created by outsiders in 2007, more than thirty thousand have appeared. Facebook couldn't possibly do all this on its own; the whole user experience is cocreated.

A radically different example that suggests even broader possibilities is described by professors C. K. Prahalad and M. S. Krishnan of the University of Michigan's Ross School of Business, who have studied and developed the idea of cocreation. Suppose the health insurance premiums of a customer with diabetes could be reset continually based on monitoring of that person's vital signs and compliance with a regimen of diet, exercise, and medication. In theory that model is possible today, and an early version is being used by ICICI Prudential Insurance in India. The service and what it costs are continually cocreated by the customer and the company in conjunction with a network of doctors, exercise facilities, and pharmaceutical firms that have joined the project.

If this sounds like the old mass-customization idea, it decidedly isn't. That concept was about a company offering customers many choices on a wide range of product or service attributes, but the company still had to decide which choices to offer and then had to deliver them. In cocreation, the choices are infinite, and the company neither imagines nor delivers them all. Similarly, if this sounds like Web 2.0, it sort of is, but it's much bigger because it's more than an Internet phenomenon.

The challenges are clear. Most companies, especially old ones, are organized exactly wrong to capitalize on cocreation. They're built around the processes of creating products and services and managing owned resources, just the opposite of the skills needed in the new model. In the same way, most managers (especially old ones) lack an intuitive feel for how the new model works. But in times that are challenging or even desperate for many companies, managers will be strongly incentivized to develop new business models that create value by using the resources of others.

Brand building in developing economies. Paulo Zegna knows all about product counterfeiting in China, but he was still surprised to see his own name being stolen. He's cochief of Ermenegildo Zegna Group, the Milan-based men's fashion house that also manufactures some of the world's best wool cloth, and a few years ago employees in southern China discovered thousands of yards of fabric with the Zegna name woven into the selvedge—but his company hadn't made it. Zegna cloth had joined the long list of products being faked in China.

A familiar tale but for one unexpected detail: instead of the low-quality rip-off you'd expect, the cloth was pretty good. Zegna won't say it matched the real thing, but it was good. And why shouldn't it be? As he told me, "The Chinese now buy the same machines as everybody else, they hire the same consultants, they compete with us to buy the same raw wool in Australia." Result: somewhere in China a company was turning out high-quality woolens worthy of being marketed under their own name, which could presumably be built into a valuable brand, yet the firm chose instead to steal someone else's name.

That sounds crazy to an increasing number of businesspeople in the developing world. It has been apparent for some time that the next great phase of business development in China and other developing economies will center on brand building, but it was slow going as long as the world clamored for low-cost manufacturing as fast as these countries could provide it. Now thousands of factories are closing, millions of factory workers are without jobs, and these countries need another, more stable, more lucrative model for prosperity.

Motivated by the current slowdown, they may become brand power-houses far more quickly than many Western companies expect. That's worrisome for today's incumbents because brands are where the money is. Brand owners typically collect most of the profit in an industry. A pair of Nike running shoes that leaves a factory in eastern China at a cost of five dollars may sell in the United States for a hundred dollars, and while Nike doesn't pocket all the difference, it pockets much more than the factory owner. The situation is the same in consumer electronics, clothing, toys, and many of the other industries in which developing economies produce most of the world output. Until recently, those nations' firms were happy to cash in on their labor-cost advantage and make more money than they'd ever seen. Now, led by companies like Lenovo (computers), Haier (appliances), TCL (consumer electronics), and others, they're going after the enormously larger sums flowing to the brand owners.

Companies in these countries may command no special brand-building talent. They possess no analog to their labor-cost advantage in manufacturing. But they do hold other advantages. They understand their home markets better than anyone else, a significant edge when those markets hold 40 percent of the world's people. And a company that builds a powerful brand in Asian markets may develop scale economies and learning-curve advantages that will strengthen it globally. For decades those phenomena helped Western companies, operating in their vast home economies, to stay on top. Now, in industries such as cell phones and PCs, where developing economies are already the world's largest market or soon will be, the tables may be turning.

We don't know all the ways the present crisis will affect companies in the developing world, but if it drives them to master the ineffable, emotional, magic power of brands, then what they've achieved so far will seem insignificant by comparison.

Imagination-based business models. As living standards decline in Western economies, a conventional response is to urge greater achievement in science and technology, long the foundation of economic dominance.

But a contrarian school argues that the whole debate is wrong—that focusing on science and technology is fighting the last war. This school holds that the very basis of value creation is shifting from the disciplines of logic and linear thinking to the intuitive, nonlinear processes of creativity and imagination. Tech advances will cease to confer much competitive advantage as they circle the world almost instantly. Authors like Daniel Pink (*A Whole New Mind*), Richard Florida (*The Rise of the Creative Class*), and Virginia Postrel (*The Substance of Style*) see the value shift happening already and say the trend is just getting started. Because it's a sharp break with past beliefs about wealth creation, the shift has been happening slowly. But now, with managers and policy makers newly open to radical-seeming solutions, it could make sudden progress.

Exhibit A in this argument is the iPod. Its success isn't based on any tech breakthrough. MP3 players had been around for years and had never done much commercially. Apple's achievement was creating an appealing design and a superior, intuitive user interface, plus the crucial business innovation of the iTunes online music store. The company then imbued the whole thing with an undeniable coolness. The result is an overwhelmingly dominant business, with about 75 percent of the MP3 player market and of the online music market—all based on existing basic technology plus a lot of ingenious creativity.

Could that model—expressed already in a thousand forms, from the carefully created Starbucks environment to Michael Graves–designed toilet brushes at Target—be the new basis of economic success? It's an extremely audacious claim. Left-brain logical rigor has been the foundation of economic growth for more than three hundred years. Most people instinctively rebel at the notion that touchy-feeliness could power great economies or even major corporations. It's fine for a few, but how can it employ the vast numbers who will no longer be working in factories, mills, and back offices?

CREATIVITY

I put that objection to Daniel Pink. He responded that in massive economic shifts, people are terrible at foreseeing what's next. The conventional view thirty years ago was that an economy couldn't be based on services—manufacturing had to be the foundation. No one "envisioned search engine optimizers or Web designers or executive coaches or nanotechnologists," he told me. "When we're cabined in the present, we suffer from a certain poverty of imagination. We massively underestimate human ingenuity and resilience." The future, he says, will bring "industries we can't imagine and jobs for which we lack the vocabulary to describe. Yes, it represents a leap of faith of sorts, but that's how it has always worked."

The vision of the right-brain future is appealing in the developed world because it plays to the West's strengths today. Some of these countries, notably the United States, are falling behind in science and math but are awesomely good at creating games, humor, design, story, emotion, and other elements of the hypothesized future. Yet the power of these right-brain creations may be highly culture specific. Indians and Chinese have right brains too—what's to stop them from charging into the economy's next phase? And don't they hold an obvious advantage in creating new industries that will dominate their own mushrooming markets?

Imagination-based business models probably don't favor any particular industry or part of the world. On the contrary, they hold the potential to disrupt almost any business and will probably be much more widely tried in an environment where, for many companies, anything is worth trying.

All three of these trends are disruptive ideas that may not have seemed worth chancing in better times. But in a deep recession, many companies have no choice but to rethink their strategies or business models, and they realize that incremental changes won't be enough to save them. As a result, many companies will embrace these trends and change their businesses significantly. Not all will succeed, but some will, and they will be among the leaders when the economy turns up.

Not every company needs to alter its strategy or business model in a recession, even a deep one. Indeed, as we've seen, one of the most important traits of the world's great companies is a strong, stable strategy that works well in all parts of the business cycle. Many work even better in a recession. Toyota's central brand promise of value and reliability is a greater advantage now than ever. Wal-Mart and Southwest Airlines typically perform great in recessions because of their low-cost strategy, and the new customers they attract in bad times tend to stay with them when good times return. Intel's towering dominance in the microprocessor business lets it increase its lead in recessions by underpricing and outlasting competitors. These fortunate outfits already possess great recession strategies.

Yet in a downturn all companies, even the best, need to reconsider strategies and business models to see if they need tweaks, refinements, or large-scale changes. In making those crucial judgments, managers must be utterly clear about the basis for their decisions—their ultimate, bottom-line objective—yet on this matter many leaders go astray, with results that can be financially fatal. Understanding the financial reality of a business in a deep recession is therefore the subject of the next chapter.

CHAPTER SEVEN

Manage for Value

Most companies don't—an error that can be fatal in this recession

The managers of a company called Varity Corporation had to make some life-or-death decisions in the recession of 1990–91. They were in the business of manufacturing farm equipment—an awful business even before the recession. It was awful because farms were consolidating and becoming more efficient, so they could squeeze more use out of each piece of equipment, and with farms increasingly owned by large corporations, they brought more buying power to the price negotiation. At the same time, the quality revolution of the 1980s had vastly extended the life of farm equipment—wonderful news for farmers and consumers, but another problem for Varity as it tried to increase sales. Then the recession landed on top of that. The company's whole future was at stake.

Desperate, the company's managers chose a path that seemed audacious at the time. They abandoned the conventional strategy of managing strictly for cash flow. Instead, they decided to manage according to a set of measures that didn't even show up in the usual financial statements. They would gauge every activity in the company by tracking how much capital it required, how much that capital cost, and whether the activity was earning more or less than the cost of the capital. Traditional income statements and balance sheets don't tell you any of this, but the managers found ways to uncover and follow their key metrics.

They discovered surprises everywhere. Lines of business that the company had valued turned out to look terrible by the new measures, so they were pruned. Manufacturing capacity that the company had considered necessary turned out not to be. Large inventories that had been regarded as prudent now looked foolish. The managers cut here, added there, and reshaped the company to make their new metrics look better.

The results were stunning. The firm's conventional financial statements, which still had to be issued, sometimes looked better and sometimes actually looked worse. But there was no confusion in the price of the stock. It went up. In fact, it more than doubled. Facing not just a recession but also large-scale problems in its industry, Varity made itself stronger and more valuable by focusing on what mattered most financially.

For every company, deciding how to measure itself in this recession is one of the most critically important decisions to be made. Yes, it's always important, but in this matter as in so many, good times can conceal a lot of sins; when the economy is growing fast, your performance is probably attractive almost any way you look at it. And yes, in a recession, when your back is to the wall and there's no room for error, every decision is important—yet this one is clearly more so. That's because the way you decide to measure your performance is the foundational decision. Once it is made, it guides virtually all your other decisions. If it's wrong, it will lead to many bad decisions, which in this environment may be disastrous.

Think of it this way. If you were sailing from Newport to Bermuda back in the days before GPS systems, and the weather was beautiful, you didn't need a perfectly precise compass heading. You'd be going in the right general direction, and if you missed Bermuda you'd probably know that because you could see it. Even if you couldn't, you had a clearly visible sun, a sharp horizon, and a steady deck, so you could easily calculate your position and then tack your way back to where you wanted to be. But in a terrible storm, your compass heading had to be perfect. If you missed Bermuda, you might not know it for a long time. With no sun, no horizon, and a heaving deck, you couldn't easily calculate your position. Even if you eventually figured out which direction to go, blasting winds and towering waves might make going that way nearly impossible.

In this recession, a violent economic storm, many managers are making life-or-death corporate decisions without a precise financial compass heading, relying instead on measures that will lead them astray. Often these managers are unclear about the most fundamental aspects of their jobs, such as what their ultimate managerial goal is and how best to achieve it. Especially in this deep recession, they are making misguided decisions about cash, debt, dividends, acquisitions, research, training, and advertising. Yet this is exactly the time when no one can afford wrong decisions, especially on such crucial matters as these.

So what's the best basis for these decisions? What's the right compass heading?

Your Real Goal

The answer isn't mysterious; it's just overlooked surprisingly often. Our system is called capitalism for a reason: it's all about capital. Yet that bedrock reality gets obscured in all kinds of ways as a result of accounting rules, corporate shorthand, media reports, and other factors. For example, many people regard a company's market capitalization as a handy measure of its success relative to other companies. A firm with a market cap of $100 billion has obviously been far more successful than one with a market cap of $20 billion. Yet if we stop and think about it, that conclusion obviously makes no sense. A company's market cap—or, more precisely, the total market value of its equity and debt, called its total enterprise value—represents the amount that investors could in theory take out of the company today. That number tells us very little, however, because it's only half the picture. To make any sense of it, we must also know the amount that investors put into the company. And once we know that, the picture can change radically.

For example, on a certain day in 2008, Time Warner and Apple happened to have total enterprise values that were almost exactly the same, a nice round $100 billion. Does that mean they had been equally successful? Let's look at the other half of the picture. Investors had put about $5 billion of capital into Apple, which had turned that capital into $100 billion of enterprise value; that is, Apple had created $95 billion of wealth. By contrast, investors had put $142 billion of capital into Time Warner, which had also turned that capital into $100 billion of enterprise value; that is, Time Warner had destroyed $42 billion of wealth. Equal enterprise values but dramatically different records of success—a reality that's obscured until we look at capital.

This example illuminates what management's ultimate goal really is, which is to create wealth, or value, as we may also call it. If that seems painfully obvious, please stop and reflect on whether you or anyone in your business is being paid explicitly for achieving that goal. In most companies, most people are paid to hit other targets— salespeople have sales quotas, plant managers have quality goals, purchasing agents have cost budgets, even the CEO may be focused on stated earnings or earnings per share. None of those goals is the same as value creation, and pursuing some of them may actually destroy value. So while it may seem obvious that every business wants to create value, many companies are managed as if that weren't true at all.

Let's be clear, therefore, on a couple of extremely basic points. Every company's goal is to create value, which means using capital to build a business that's worth more than the capital itself. And the way this is done—similarly simple—is to earn a return on the capital that's greater than the cost of the capital, a measure that financial economists call economic profit. If that also seems painfully obvious, consider that no standard financial statement as mandated by the accounting rules of any nation will tell you if a company is accomplishing this. Yet that's what it's all about—as every independent businessperson understands viscerally. A woman selling fruit on the street in Mumbai knows exactly how much capital she's using, in the form of working capital used to purchase her inventory of fruit. She knows what it costs because she borrowed it from a loan shark. And she understands intensely that if she's to support herself and her family, she needs to earn more than the cost of that capital.

Get to Know Your Capital

That's the most basic rule of business, and it applies equally to the Indian fruit vendor and to the largest corporations on earth. Many of the world's best-managed companies understand this rule and live by it, but many other companies don't. The resulting wrong decisions may be survivable in a growing economy, but, as we shall see, they can be fatal in a deep recession. To understand exactly how, we must first explore two simple questions:

How much capital is in our business? The short answer is, probably much more than you think. It's easy to identify the classic forms of capital—land, buildings, machinery, vehicles. Most businesses also require working capital, what Adam Smith called "circulating capital," the money that's always in use to pay for inventories and otherwise keep the business operating. And capital is obviously tied up when a company buys another company; if the price is greater than the stated value of the target company's assets, then the difference is capital that the accountants call goodwill.

But if you think that's all the capital in your business, you're probably underestimating. Much confusion and trouble arises from the accounting rules on this matter. The rules say, for example, that any money you spend on research and development is an expense, not an investment, so your R & D spending doesn't increase the amount of capital invested in your company. But in reality, we all know that's crazy. Of course your R & D spending is an investment: it will pay off years from now, and the benefits will last for many years thereafter. The accountants, in their well-intended zeal to be conservative, won't let you acknowledge that reality in your official financial statements, but it's still reality. That is, the money you spend on R & D is actually increasing the total capital invested in your firm.

Several other types of expenses are similar. How about marketing? For some firms, brands are the most valuable assets they own. Roberto Goizueta, former CEO of Coca-Cola, was fond of pointing out that if every physical asset the company owned were to burn to the ground tomorrow, the company could immediately borrow all the money it needed to rebuild simply on the value of the Coca-Cola brand. Accounting rules say the marketing expenditures that built this megabrand weren't investments, yet obviously they were.

It's the same story with employee training and development—clearly an investment, considering that the benefits will last for years. Spending money to entice customers from a competitor is another example of an investment that by accounting rules must be called an expense.

Of course you must abide by the rules in issuing financial statements. But for your own internal purposes, to guide managerial decisions, you can keep the books as you like. And to make the best decisions in a deep recession, it's vital that you acknowledge the financial reality of how much capital you have truly invested in your business, and where.

How much does our capital really cost? Many people think this one's easy to answer: we pay interest on our debt, so that must be the cost of our capital. But as all finance wonks know, it isn't so. Your business uses two kinds of capital, debt and equity, and the equity's cost—while not in the form of cash—is actually quite high. It's equal to the return that an equity investor could get in some other investment that's as risky as investing in your company; after all, that's what you're asking investors to give up in order to place their capital with your business, so you'd better be able to match it. If you can't, then your business isn't justifying its existence financially.

Equity investments are riskier than debt investments because under the law, debt holders get paid before equity holders; to compensate for that extra risk, equity capital is more expensive than debt. (In addition, debt generally gets a tax advantage because interest payments are tax deductible.) Your company's real cost of capital is the weighted average of the costs of these two components. For example, if your cost of debt is 10 percent and your cost of equity is 14 percent, and you use them in equal amounts, then your cost of capital is 12 percent.

Massive books have been written on precisely how to calculate the cost of capital, but don't let the perfect be the enemy of the good. If you're in a small business, you may never have made this calculation. For you, embracing the concept and getting a rough idea of the correct value is far more important than being exactly right. If you're in a giant company, your CFO knows the firm's cost of capital—but how many other people do? Considering how important it is, especially during a steep downturn, everyone should.

Making the Right Decisions the Right Way

With those concepts firmly in mind, how should managers make the crucial decisions that face them in this recession? We have the correct compass heading. Now how do we make sure the boat is proceeding directly on it? We'll find the answers by examining the decisions managers are making now in three major categories.

Deciding what to manage for. Perhaps the most ancient cliché about recession managing says, "Cash is king." It's true—up to a point. When times are genuinely tough, just paying the bills can be a problem for some companies. If you can't make payroll, nothing else matters. Such concerns have affected far more companies than usual in this recession, partly because the downturn is so severe, but also because parts of the capital markets shut down as they have never done before. Many companies, including big, famous ones, relied on the commercial paper market for the cash to handle their day-to-day transactions. That market stopped operating for a while after the collapse of Lehman Brothers in September 2008, and suddenly even companies that never had to worry about how much cash was in the bank found themselves intensely worried about it. For these companies, the simple basics of cash management—collecting it as quickly as possible and paying it as slowly as possible—became critical management competencies.

Believe it or not, those are new skills for some companies, outfits that are managed for reported earnings. Such firms want to maximize the number at the bottom of their income statement, calculated by the rules of accounting—which sounds reasonable until we realize the trouble it can cause. Accounting rules increase or decrease reported profits in all kinds of ways that have zero effect on cash moving into or out of the firm. An extreme example is what Enron used to do perfectly legally. It would sign a twenty-year contract to provide services of some kind to another company, then calculate the present value of that twenty-year stream of income and report the whole thing as revenue during the quarter in which the contract was signed—creating a huge reported profit but putting almost no money in the bank. Enron seemed to be performing financial wonders until the recession of 2001 forced a focus on real money.

So it's easy to see why companies that have been managing for reported earnings become fervent converts to the doctrine of managing for cash in a recession. The trouble is, just as their earlier obsession wasn't correct, their new one isn't either. Remember, the thing for which we're ultimately managing our businesses isn't reported earnings or cash; it's value. It turns out that managing for cash—though everyone seems to recommend it in a recession—can gravely damage value.

The reason is clear when we recall our earlier discussion about capital. If a manager's assignment is simply to conserve cash, he'll probably cut spending in areas where it's easiest to do: marketing, employee training, research. Those are expenditures that can be turned on or off quickly. But if we think of them as what they really are—capital investments—we realize that cutting them may actually destroy value. That is, if those were investments that made sense when properly analyzed, meaning they generated a return on capital exceeding the cost of the capital, then they probably still make sense. So cutting them would still destroy value, which is a bad thing to do, even in a recession.

To which a desperate manager will respond, *I need* cash—*what am I supposed to do?* Fortunately, companies that decide to manage for value almost always uncover lots of cash that they never realized was available. For example, they typically discover mountains of inventory, representing capital sitting in warehouses. When they understand how much that capital costs, they find ways to reduce inventories, yielding a massive, one-time jolt of newly available cash. They also find that operating with leaner inventories saves cash every day as they pay less for space, warehouse employees, and other costs.

Even those "one-time" benefits from reducing inventories can be recurring. It's remarkable how companies that focus on running leaner can keep finding new ways to do it. Wal-Mart, one of the few businesses to do well in this recession, has been trying to squeeze inventories for more than forty years. Yet in its fiscal 2009, even as revenues increased, it managed to shrink inventories, thus increasing its cash flow.

Companies that are managed for value generally become far more cash efficient in other ways as well. Because they see all assets as capital with a cost, they find innovative ways to operate with less capital and to generate the greatest return for what they've got. When Dell revolutionized the personal computer business in the 1990s, for example, it did so with a clear, value-based strategy, finding ingenious ways to operate with minimal inventories and maximum speed. Consider Dell's cash conversion cycle, which many companies try valiantly to shorten during a recession; it's the number of days that elapse between paying for the components of what a company makes and receiving cash from the customer for the product in which those components are used. Dell got its cash conversion cycle down to an incredible negative eight days: when you ordered a computer, they collected your money eight days before they paid the suppliers of the components.

Managing for value frees up cash in still more ways. Companies may find that certain offices, plants, or lines of business aren't earning their cost of capital and have no prospect of doing so. They can (and should) be shut down or sold. In this recession, when cash seems so especially dear, managing for value may show the way to finding additional cash that wasn't available prerecession. That's because credit markets have seized up and made the short-term cost of capital higher than it used to be, at least for many firms. As managers evaluate operations against the standard of a higher capital cost, they will likely find that some no longer meet the test and should be stopped, thus freeing up more cash.

No one disputes that many companies have to go looking for cash in a recession. The challenge is finding it in the right places, which are frequently not the places where most companies look. If your prerecession spending on marketing or R & D made sense when analyzed for value, then continuing it now could represent a huge competitive advantage—because less enlightened firms will slash such investments. Many managers worry that the stock market may punish them for spending on such items during a recession, but research shows persuasively that it won't. On the contrary, investors understand that these items are investments, not expenses. Nick Calamos, the highly regarded mutual fund manager, told us at *Fortune* that in analyzing a company he always capitalizes R & D, for example, meaning he regards it as an investment. Studies by Baruch Lev of New York University have led him to conclude, "Despite widespread allegations of stock market 'short-termism' . . . the research indicates unequivocally that capital markets consider investments in R&D as a significant value-increasing activity." The same holds true for all capital investments, regardless of how they must be classified for accounting purposes: if they're creating value, try your hardest to avoid cutting them.

Mergers and acquisitions. Merger activity typically plunges in a recession, and that has been happening this time. The reasons are simple. Many potential acquirers don't want to spend cash on deals because they feel they must conserve it for paying the day-to-day bills. They may not be able to borrow much money in today's slowly thawing capital markets. And they hesitate to use their stock as currency because it's worth so much less than it was just a year or two ago. On the other side, potential sellers don't want to sell unless they're desperate, because their companies would today fetch only a fraction of what they were worth in the good times.

Yet a historic downturn is a terrific opportunity for companies to buy other firms at bargain prices, and it can even work out well for sellers. The key is remembering that any deal is a capital investment intended to create value.

Extensive research has shown that most acquisitions fail— meaning they fail to increase the wealth of the acquiring shareholders. Why? Analysts love to talk about strategic fit and cultural compatibility, but the most common reason is much more basic: the acquiring company paid too much. Once that mistake is made, there's no way out. Earlier we looked at Time Warner, a champion wealth destroyer. Years ago, as Time Inc., the company was an outstanding wealth creator. What happened was the AOL–Time Warner merger, one of the highest-priced mergers of all time. The mammoth price represented a staggering sum of capital invested in the new enterprise, on which the company has never been able to earn a satisfactory return. Investors are still suffering almost a decade later.

Deals that make financial sense should be done in bad times as well as good, yet often they are not. The reasons, mentioned above, are generally not valid ones. Logical thinking for parties on either side of a potential transaction goes as follows.

For potential buyers: Don't have enough cash to buy the target companies you'd like, and can't get it in today's dislocated capital markets? Then use your stock as your currency. The fact that it's worth much less than it used to be is irrelevant. The companies you're thinking of buying are also worth much less, so the exchange ratio may not have changed. And don't worry about diluting your earnings per share by issuing new stock for the deal. Your alternative—using cash, which must be supplied or replaced through borrowing—increases your company's leverage and thus its risk, which reduces its price-earnings multiple. Research has shown that in using stock as your currency, what you sacrifice in dilution you recoup through a higher multiple. So deals at a sensible price are still doable.

For potential sellers: Hate the idea of selling at today's battered prices? The hard reality is that yesterday's price has no bearing on the best decision for today. Yes, you'll receive much less than you could have received a few years ago. But when you reinvest the proceeds, you'll be able to buy much more than you could have bought. If you have an opportunity to sell, the question you should be asking is stated clearly by Bennett Stewart, CEO of the EVA Dimensions consulting firm and a pioneer in applying these concepts: "Would the after-tax sale proceeds, reinvested at the cost of capital, provide more earnings than the business provides? If so, then a sale makes sense."

Acquisitions don't become a bad idea in a bad economy. The opportunity is to think about them correctly—through the lens of capital—at a time when the thinking of others is muddled.

Dividends. Most companies that pay dividends hate reducing them, yet that's what many have been doing. Most dramatic was General Electric's decision to cut its dividend for the first time in seventy-one years, and not just trim it, but whack it by two-thirds. The same painful move had already been made by other aristocrats of the corporate world: JPMorgan Chase, Dow Chemical, Pfizer, and the New York Times Company. Overall, dividends paid by the S&P 500 dropped to at least a fifty-year low.

Yet it's possible that those companies have been forced into doing something smart. Paying a dividend achieves nothing for shareholders. It merely gives them some money that they already hold, embodied in the price of the stock. Every time a company pays a dividend, the price of its stock drops by the amount of the dividend. Moving the money from the company's bank account into the shareholder's bank account creates no value; instead it destroys value, because the shareholder must pay tax on the income. Especially at a time when taxes on dividends are likely to rise in the United States and other developed economies, cutting dividends—or even eliminating them—looks smart. And for companies seeking value-friendly ways to increase cash, this one is hard to beat.

A wonderful thing about the principles of finance is that they don't change. In a deep downturn, when every company must operate within much narrower margins of error, observing them becomes much more critical. Yet many managers, disoriented by the unfamiliar conditions, lose sight of the basic principles at just this crucial moment. The opportunity is to chart a course that may seem contrarian—to avoid cutting costs that others are cutting, to do deals that others won't do—secure in the knowledge that you're actually pointed in the right direction, and when the storm ends, you'll be far ahead of your competitors.

CHAPTER EIGHT

Create New Solutions for Customers' New Problems

You can do it in more ways than you may realize

Luxury was not selling well in the first holiday season of this reces-sion, and Saks Fifth Avenue was feeling the pain. The suffering couldn't be avoided. Luxury is the foundation of the store's whole identity. It's said in New York City that society ladies on Manhattan's Upper East Side once had a firm rule, and some still do, never to travel south of Fiftieth Street—except to enter Saks, which spans Fifth Av-enue's eastern flank from Fiftieth to Forty-ninth streets. Epitomizing luxury had served Saks well for decades, but now that glittering iden-tity had become a big problem.

Responding radically, Saks cut prices on many products by 40 percent, a deep reduction that no retailer likes to make and that lux-ury retailers especially hate because in their world, a product's tower-ing price is one of its key attributes. Maybe that's one reason the price cuts weren't working, at least not well enough. As November proceeded and the merchandise wasn't moving, Saks took the unprec-edented step of cutting prices an additional 50 percent, for a total price drop of 70 percent. The resulting prices were more than just low; they were disorienting. A Valentino evening dress that had been offered at $2,950 was now marked $885. A Prada satchel that had been $1,920 was $575.95. Jimmy Choo Hallie knee-high boots that were $1,195 had been reduced to $358.45. The retail world was reeling. Those prices on those products in that store had never been seen before.

A few blocks away, a different luxury retailer was following a markedly different strategy. Jay Kos is a Park Avenue shop that sells high-end men's clothing to finance moguls, media celebrities, and other elite New Yorkers. In the autumn of 2008, as Saks was slicing prices, this shop covered its window with newspaper headlines about the collapsing economy, then posted its own announcements over that background: "Cashmere sweater: $2,500. Recession price: $2,500." "Lamb's fleece jacket: $11,000. Recession price: $11,000." It was an in-your-face declaration that this business wouldn't be caving in to any mere economic disaster.

And the results? Saks Inc.'s December sales dropped 20 percent, a terrible performance; perhaps even worse, the company may have done long-term damage to its valuable brand, as we'll discuss shortly. As for Jay Kos's approach, "Some people hated it," the shop's eponymous owner told me. "But most people loved it. And some people even bought because of it."

Saks Fifth Avenue and Jay Kos are in the same business of luxury retailing, serving the same customers in the same place, yet they drew radically different conclusions about how consumers would behave in today's economy. It would be foolish to speculate on how each business will ultimately fare; many factors will determine that. The important point is that every company is being forced to answer the same fundamental question that these businesses faced, and as their differing strategies show, the correct answer isn't obvious. Yet choosing an answer—deciding exactly how (or even whether) to alter the firm's offer to its customers in response to a downturn—is one of the most important decisions a company can make.

The decision is difficult because the many ways in which customers behave differently during a recession are not simple or obvious. As we saw in chapter 6, customers will reduce spending on some items but will actually spend more on others. Those decisions may not always seem logical. Does it really make sense to spend more on going to movies during a recession? Or to buy at a hyperexpensive men's shop just because it proclaimed a defiant attitude?

Complicating the decision further, there's good reason to believe that customers are deviating even from their usual recession patterns this time around. The extraordinary debt they've piled up in the United States, the UK, and other economies has left them less able to spend their already reduced incomes. The abnormally rapid annihilation of jobs around the world has rendered consumers extremely wary of making long-term commitments, such as mortgages, and of committing to anything very far in advance. In addition, since this recession is accelerating several trends that were already under way, it's likely that many of the disappearing jobs will not be coming back when the economy recovers. Manufacturing jobs that are being vaporized in developed economies will eventually be replaced by a smaller number of new jobs in developing economies. All those newspapers that are shutting down are not going to start back up when times get better. The world will need more investment bankers someday, but those jobs won't be the same when they return. As a result, an unusually large number of consumers are thinking about changing careers, living in new places, or maybe being unemployed for a very long time—all of which changes their wants, needs, and actions. Responding to customers in any recession is hard enough, but it's yet another imperative that's even harder this time because experience may not tell us much.

Never Stop Experimenting

To meet this challenge at a time when nothing seems constant, it's vital to remember what hasn't changed and won't change. Most fun-

[handwritten margin note: THE FUTURE WILL NOT BE A RETURN OF THE PAST.]

damentally, every company offers its customers not just a product or service but a value proposition, and that value proposition consists of a complete customer experience (a concept on which the consultant Michael J. Lanning has written extensively). The experience comprises many parts, of which price is only one. To take an example from a particularly troubled industry, consider the value propositions offered by automakers. The experience includes choosing the model and options you want, negotiating the price, perhaps arranging the financing, taking delivery, driving the vehicle, getting it serviced, possibly arranging repairs under the warranty, and probably trading it in—and each of those elements is a multipart experience as well. Overall it's an experience that spans years, yet in a recession many carmakers seem to believe that only one element, price, matters to potential customers.

The most successful companies understand that through good times and bad, they're always creating complete experiences to meet their customers' changing wants and needs. The process doesn't start when a recession hits. Instead, these companies are constantly monitoring the state of their customers and are experimenting with new value propositions that could better serve customers. That process, rigorously pursued, accounts for a good deal of Amazon's success, for example. Its online business model allows it to test new value propositions quickly and easily, say by altering the shipping options it offers or by fine-tuning the checkout process. The company typically tries such experiments on carefully chosen subsets of customers, and it tries them on a scale that would stun most companies—frequently conducting three hundred different experiments per day. Sometimes it gets statistically significant results within hours and can roll out the altered experience company-wide before the day is over.

You don't need Amazon's business model in order to benefit from the same general practice. For example, Seven-Eleven Japan has for years been a champion at experimenting, learning, and adjusting its customer experiences accordingly. Employees at every level understand that it's part of their job. On a typical morning, a part-time employee at a Tokyo store in this major chain of convenience retailers notices that the weather is forecast to be much chillier than the previous two days, so he increases his store's order for lunchtime hot noodles and cuts the order for cold noodles—at a time when the order typically didn't change from day to day. By afternoon, the experiment was proven successful. Obvious? Maybe—but it was news to busy store managers who were focused on other things.

Now imagine the power of Amazon's three hundred value proposition experiments every day or of hundreds of Seven-Eleven Japan stores continually trying such experiments and sharing the results with headquarters every week. Changes in customer behavior, even in a severe recession, come as no surprise to these outfits. And imagine the advantage these firms hold over competitors that don't conduct these experiments, haven't built up the resulting massive trove of customer knowledge, and don't possess such a customer-focused culture. Those companies are flailing in this recession.

Did It Work?

The best companies go even further: they create different value propositions for different customers or customer segments. For example, the consumer electronics retailer Best Buy has famously segmented its customers into several groups to which it offers markedly different value propositions. In the last recession the company found that some of these segments, such as home theater aficionados, were highly profitable and scarcely cut back their spending. So the company shifted resources to serving these segments better and came out of the recession stronger than it went in. During the current recession Best Buy has held up well, while its principal direct competitor, Circuit City, filed for bankruptcy protection and closed all its stores.

In judging value propositions, deciding whether experiments

were successes to be scaled up, the most successful companies remember the real bottom line. As we discussed in the previous chapter, it's economic profit. In most companies the deeply entrenched tradition is to evaluate customer initiatives on some other criterion: gross margin, market share, customer satisfaction, customer retention, or any of a dozen other measures. Those measures may be important, but ultimately they aren't good enough, because you can increase every one of them in ways that reduce economic profit and destroy shareowner value. For example, you can build gross margin by making capital investments that reduce labor costs but don't generate a satisfactory return on the capital used; it works because the capital costs aren't included in gross margin. You can buy market share with price cuts. You can increase customer satisfaction and retention through all sorts of giveaways to the customer that will cost shareholders dearly.

▶ Only by looking at changes in economic profit for a customer segment can a firm make a sound judgment about the success of a value-proposition experiment—and such calculations are indeed possible. The process may require making some assumptions (about the average length of customer relationships, for example, or capital allocation), but as a company repeats the process over time, it will accumulate data that will turn those assumptions into numbers used with ever greater confidence. (For a much more detailed explanation of these concepts, you may want to check out a book I cowrote with the consultant and professor Larry Selden, *Angel Customers and Demon Customers*.) And even when the calculation has to be based on assumptions or estimates, it's still the right calculation to be making.

Getting Creative in Meeting New Needs

As companies create new value propositions for their customers' new recessionary wants and needs, they can do so on several dimensions, giving companies more options than many managers may realize.

● The simplest approach to creating a recession value proposition is devising a new product or service that offers the customer a reduced experience, carefully defined, at a lower price. For example, Verizon Communications is worried that the recession may spur some customers to cancel their landline phones and switch to services being offered by cable TV companies, or to just rely on their cell phones. Landlines are enormously profitable for Verizon even when customers pay low prices, so the company may offer customers a plan that permits calls only to 911 and Verizon customer service, at a price of five dollars a month. The attraction for customers is peace of mind: when electric power fails, cable service doesn't work and cell phones can't be charged, but landlines still operate. That new value proposition may appeal to some customer segments while earning money for Verizon.

The same principle works in any business if applied with care. When the economy was strong, CKE Restaurants, parent of the Hardee's and Carl's Jr. chains, developed a winning strategy based on massive burgers—sometimes with sliced steak or pastrami on top— at premium prices. When the recession hit, many customers balked at paying those prices. For CKE, responding with a new value proposition of skinny burgers at bargain prices would have destroyed the market position that it had built over years, so it responded more carefully. "We can't add meat to a burger anymore," said CKE marketing chief Brad Haley, since the cost is too high for the company and for its customers. "We have to be more creative. Carl's Jr. is promoting a guacamole bacon cheeseburger. Avocados are a less expensive topping." The burgers are still big, and that bit of bacon still gives consumers just a little extra meat on the burger—preserving the company's brand positioning—but the price is slightly lower, and CKE still makes a profit.

An innovative variation on this theme uses clever partnering strategies. In the grocery business, private-label products already represent the reduced-offering-at-a-lower-price strategy. Unsurprisingly, consumers have flocked to them in this recession. Sales of private-label consumer products jumped 10 percent in the United States in 2008, while sales of branded products increased only 2.8 percent. That's great for the big grocery chains that sell these private-label goods, but how can the big brand owners—Kraft Foods, General Mills, Sara Lee, and many others—compete? Several have teamed with major retailers, who are not only their private-label competitors but also their biggest customers, to create new value propositions that help them both. General Mills offers retailers a "pizza night" display that features General Mills pizza dough and the retailer's private-label tomato products. The promotion offers consumers a money-saving meal option—make pizza at home using economical private-label tomato sauce, instead of ordering from a pizza shop—while still selling General Mills branded dough. Kraft Foods has created sandwich promotions along similar lines—use Kraft meat and cheese, they tell consumers, between slices of private-label bread from the retailer.

Those tactics work because in a recession, consumers may be willing to make do with a little less in order to pay a little less; private-label products might not be quite as good as the big brands, or offer the same degree of confidence, but they're good enough for now. Yet in other settings there may be no trade-off at all; that is, a wise company may be able to create a new value proposition that asks the customer to make no sacrifices. For example, McKinsey reports that when the economy was booming, a client company that sells plastic resins developed a fast-curing resin for customers who wanted maximum productivity from their injection-molding machines. The resin was expensive but worth it. When the economy turned down and clients no longer needed as much output from their machines, the company developed a less expensive, slower curing resin. No trade-off: customers met their new requirements fully at a lower per-unit cost. They were happy because their costs had fallen; and because the new product cost less to make, the chemical company maintained its profit margins even when selling at a lower price.

A different category of response to this recession involves giving customers more control. Because consumers are so particularly uncertain about their future, and are thus less willing to make purchases that involve commitments, they like new value propositions that give them a way out if they need it. A striking example came from Hyundai. When most of its major competitors were focusing on only one part of the customer experience by cutting prices furiously, Hyundai offered U.S. consumers a different value proposition that was entirely original in its industry: buy one of our cars, and if you can't make the payments any time in the following year, you can give the car back to us, and we'll cancel the debt. Consumers loved the idea that they wouldn't be locked into a commitment. In the first month of the new value proposition, U.S. sales of most carmakers fell by historic proportions—32 percent at Toyota, 40 percent at Ford, 49 percent at General Motors, 55 percent at Chrysler. Sales of exactly one company rose by double digits: Hyundai, up 14 percent—without even talking about price.

Players in a completely different industry are using the same idea. Traditional cell phone calling plans require customers to make a two-year commitment, which millions of them no longer want to do. In response, several companies are creating innovative prepaid plans that require no commitment. You pay for each month in advance, and each month you can change to a different, more appealing plan or pay nothing at all. Note that prepaid calling requires a significant trade-off: you have to buy your phone outright rather than pay for it indirectly at a subsidized price, as you do with a traditional plan. But many customers are happy to make that trade-off in order to get total control over their monthly mobile phone expenses. By the time the recession was well under way at the end of 2008, prepaid services were growing three times faster than traditional services.

Prepaid calling isn't necessarily a threat to incumbent wireless service providers. On the contrary, it's an excellent illustration of the benefits available through creating different value propositions to meet the needs of different customer segments. For customers who especially prize convenience, traditional plans still make sense. For those who now want maximum control, prepaid plans are a better option. The major service providers subsegment both groups and offer long menus of choices.

And yet—sometimes don't you have to just plain cut your price? The answer is yes, but those times are far rarer than most businesspeople seem to think. Every company is facing difficult decisions about pricing in this recession, and those decisions will be among the most far-reaching. Yet they're often made hastily and based on instinct, without an understanding of their potentially thundering repercussions. The topic is so important that the next chapter is devoted to it.

CHAPTER NINE

Price with Courage

Don't assume you have to mark down—it's riskier than you may think

If you sell crude oil or other commodities that are traded around the clock in global markets, then your price is set by others; you have no choice. If you sell branded products at retail or wholesale and have chosen to position your business as the low-price vendor, then you obviously have to match competitors' prices (or change your positioning). But if you aren't in either of those situations, then cutting prices, even in a recession, may not be nearly as wise a move as you think. Do think about it carefully, because it's one of the more momentous decisions you will make. You'll be living with the effects long after this recession is over.

To say that price cuts aren't inevitable in a recession is an understatement. Several highly successful companies have actually raised prices in this recession. All three of the major consumer packaged goods companies—Colgate-Palmolive, Procter & Gamble, and Unilever—raised prices in 2008, when the U.S. recession was well under way. They all said they were doing it in response to higher raw material costs, and no doubt that was true. When oil was at $145 a barrel, all kinds of plastics and chemicals used by these companies became sharply more expensive. But when commodity prices plunged in late 2008, these companies did not cut back their prices. In fact, Unilever raised prices more than 9 percent in the year's fourth quarter. Exactly how these companies managed to raise prices in such a miserable economic environment is a question we'll examine shortly, but for the moment just note that they sell commonplace household products, not rare goods with mysterious properties. And as of this writing they've all outperformed the stock market during this recession.

Yet few managerial decisions are more common in a recession than cutting prices. If you believe that you absolutely must do it, please consider fully all the potential dangers, which are much more extensive than many businesspeople imagine.

Price cuts rarely pay for themselves. They may even reduce profit more than holding prices steady would do. The math is simple: if you cut prices by 20 percent, you have to sell 25 percent more units just to maintain revenue. In most businesses that's asking a lot. Is your market really full of customers who will buy that much more in response to a price cut, especially during this recession? If competitors match your price cut, will it generate any additional sales at all? And remember, such a blowout increase in sales would be necessary just to achieve steady revenues; to maintain profits would require an even greater sales jump. The economics of every business are different, but McKinsey research finds that in a typical S&P 1500 company, a price cut of only 5 percent would have to generate increased sales volume of 19 percent in order to pay for itself. That almost never happens.

The implication is that while holding prices steady may cause sales and profits to decline somewhat, that course may nonetheless be wiser. It all depends on the pricing dynamics in your business, which may be changing rapidly in this recession. For example, record high gasoline prices in mid-2008 caused many consumers to cut back drastically on discretionary purchases; when gas prices then fell by 60 percent or more, many consumers found they had more available income—but they were also more worried about their jobs because that's just when the employment situation grew suddenly worse. Now is the time to study price sensitivity in your markets much more closely than before. Also more frequently—research won't be helpful for more than a few months.

● It's bad enough that price cuts almost never pay for themselves directly and may reduce profits below what they'd be if you held prices steady. That's only the beginning of the damage that can be done by price cutting. The possible indirect effects are potentially much worse. For example:

Price cuts can destroy brand equity that took years to build and may take years to restore. The most extreme cases recently have involved luxury products, as described in the previous chapter. Marketers of these products spend enormous energy and resources creating the perception that they're worth what they cost—that a combination of superior design, quality materials, exquisite workmanship, rarity, and a carefully crafted aura of desirability make, say, an Hermès Birkin handbag, not quite fourteen inches long, worth seven thousand dollars or more. It's sort of a magic spell that maintains its power as long as enough people believe in it.

The problem with price cuts is that they break the spell. Consider that Valentino evening dress, normally $2,950, that Saks was offering for $885. The customer's unavoidable reaction will be to ask, What is a Valentino dress, really? If I can buy it for $885—and buy it at that price not as a secondhand garment at a thrift shop, or a year out of date at some outlet mall in the woods of Maine, but here in midtown Manhattan at a temple of upscale retailing—then why was it ever worth $2,950? What is the meaning of that brand, and is it really as valuable as I used to believe? Similar thoughts surely run through the head of any customer who paid $2,950 for the dress a few months earlier; such a person probably feels foolish and may resolve not to make that mistake again.

The phenomenon has affected much more than just a few brands at Saks. Many luxury brands and luxury retailers cut prices deeply in this recession, and they realize the implications may be game changing. That's why Valérie Hermann, CEO of YSL—which cut prices about 50 percent at its own boutique in Manhattan—told us at *Fortune*, "This is a crisis of values."

Purveyors of luxe understand the dangers of price cutting and sometimes try to cut prices more subtly. For example, the recession has hurt luxury hotels badly, but if they reduce their rates, then what are they? As the manager of a Boston luxury hotel told the *New York Times*, "We don't want to discount to the extent that we reposition ourselves into a different segment, and wake up one day a year from now saying, 'Oops, we're no longer a luxury hotel.'" To avoid that fate, some are trying different tactics. A tasteful ad for Four Seasons Hotels and Resorts says, "Two days to see so much. Might we treat you to a day to recover?" That is, three nights for the price of two—a price cut in different clothes. Ritz-Carlton has offered multinight deals that include a $140 "resort credit" that can be applied to meals, spa treatments, and other services—another way to reduce the customer's bill without cutting the rate.

Yet even these tactics aren't very effective when those hotels negotiate with large corporate purchasers, who aren't fooled by sleight of hand and just focus on the bottom-line price. If it goes down, they'll remember it, which is part of another problem.

Price cuts train customers to behave badly. Buyers of all kinds have a tendency to remember the lowest price they ever paid for your product or service. In pricing theory that's known as the "reference price" because customers compare all future prices against it. The implicit question you'll always have to answer is If I got it for X, why should I ever pay more? If you haven't got a good answer, then you may have to drop the price back down to X to generate sales. That has been the story in the U.S. major-appliance industry. When manufacturers discount prices, sales spike, then drop to low levels when prices return to nonpromotional levels, according to research from Accenture. Customers are learning to buy only when these products are discounted.

Even a single price reduction can cause a problem, because customers may wonder if it's part of a new pattern. Frank Luby, a pricing specialist with the Simon-Kucher consulting firm, told me that the danger is "a halo effect—people will expect a discount later, even though a company hasn't done it yet." They may wait for it a long time.

Breaking a pattern of price cuts is even harder than it may seem because . . .

Customers hate price increases more than they like price cuts. This is one of the principle findings of behavioral finance, what the researchers call "loss aversion." Human beings are much more sensitive to losses than to equivalent gains; winning $100 makes us feel good, but losing $100 makes us feel very, very bad. From a customer's perspective, a price increase is a loss. So when you cut your product's price from $1,000 to $800, the customer was happy, but $800 became his reference price. When you try to return the price to $1,000, the customer feels as if you're killing him.

An additional factor complicates the problem. It's just simple math, and it shouldn't really make any difference, but it does. When you cut a price from $1,000 to $800, that's a 20 percent cut. But when you return the price to $1,000, that's a 25 percent increase. You're only getting back to where you started, but a 25 percent increase sounds like a lot. The greater the original discount, the bigger the problem. Recovering a 10 percent price cut takes only an 11 percent increase. But recovering a 40 percent discount requires a 67 percent increase. Recovering a 70 percent price cut will mean imposing a 233 percent price increase, and you can imagine how customers will respond to that. Thus, in addition to all the other problems that price cutting can cause, it also creates a trap that's terribly difficult to escape.

Consider all those possible consequences, and you can see why Frank Luby says, "Deep discounting is incredibly destructive." Price cutting is obvious and easy to do, and many managers do it reflexively in a downturn, not thinking through all the implications. You may feel that you must, and maybe you're right. But—are you sure?

How Much Pricing Power Do You Really Have?

Pricing is a continuing process through good times and bad. It's just that in good times you probably don't have to get it exactly right, while in a serious recession the stakes are much higher. To help understand how companies price any product or service in this environment, it helps to consider a simple two-dimensional matrix.

On one axis is how differentiated the customer considers the product or service to be, ranging from an undifferentiated commodity at one extreme to an utterly unique offering at the opposite end. On the other axis is how strongly the customer feels a need for the product or service, from considering it a must-have at one end to seeing it as totally discretionary at the other. Where do various products and services—including yours—land on this matrix?

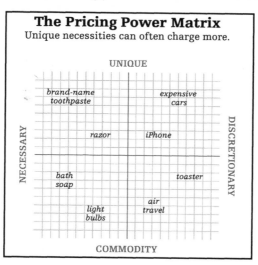

The Pricing Power Matrix
Unique necessities can often charge more.

The best spot is the corner representing a unique necessity; the customer has gotta have it, and no close substitutes exist. When we ponder which products might occupy this rich territory, we begin to understand how the consumer packaged goods companies have been able to raise prices even in this recession. An excellent example of a product in this favored corner of the matrix is Colgate toothpaste. Few people will stop brushing their teeth, no matter how bad the recession gets, and personal care brand preferences are deeply ingrained; that's why Colgate has been able to raise prices, and it's an important part of why the company's profits rose in 2008 and were forecast to increase smartly in 2009. Many of the products sold by Colgate, P&G, and Unilever share these traits: they satisfy basic needs; they carry strong brands; they involve personal care and thus connect deeply with the consumer; and they perform at least as well as any competitor. It helps that many of them are not purchased very often; you probably don't remember the last time you bought toothpaste or what it cost. That combination leads to pricing paradise.

Conversely, the worst locale on the matrix is the opposite corner, where we find discretionary commodities; one competitor is much like another, and at any given moment most people don't really need any of them. In this miserable spot sit many major airlines. Much travel can be postponed, and customers find little reason to choose one carrier over another on heavily traveled routes. The contrast with the consumer packaged goods companies is striking. Both industries raised prices in mid-2008 as oil rose to $145 a barrel. But the Colgates of the world were able to maintain their new prices when oil came back down, while airlines, caught in the opposite corner of the pricing matrix, had to drop their prices in lockstep. By 2009 they were offering some of the lowest fares seen in years. It's an old story; with essentially no pricing power, airlines frequently get into price wars in which everyone loses. That's exactly what happened to them in the last recession, and they've done it again this time.

U.S. carmakers occupy the same corner; you can probably use

your current car for another year, and if you do decide to buy a new one, the brand strength of the U.S. makers is generally much weaker than the imports. General Motors insisted it would not repeat its employee-discount price-cutting promotion of several years ago, but in this recession it did exactly that, which of course did not deliver the company from its desperate straits.

The other two corners of the matrix represent in-between cases. Must-have commodities are items like lightbulbs and toilet paper; no one will stop buying them, but the brands don't carry much power. Highly differentiated discretionary purchases are products like a Rolls-Royce; it's unique, but nobody actually needs one. Neither category commands much pricing power in a recession.

The most important insight into pricing is that smart companies use tools like this matrix not to analyze products or services, but to analyze customers. The matrix is based entirely on customer perceptions, which vary widely, so for any product or service that you sell, you must consider not one matrix but several—one for each of your customer segments. For example, you and I might consider that Rolls-Royce entirely unnecessary, but there may exist a segment of customers who feel they cannot exist without one. Failing to differentiate that segment from others would be missing a giant opportunity. In general, knowing where your product or service falls on the matrices of various customer segments—and how its location has changed as a result of the recession—enables you to create different value propositions in which price will play a greater or lesser role. The principle applies to any kind of offering, not just high-end products. McKinsey reports, for example, that a beverage company found price sensitivity varied by a factor of three just across zip codes within Jacksonville, Florida. Offering all of them the same price wouldn't make much sense.

Every part of a business gets stressed in a deep recession, and all parts are connected. Getting pricing even a little bit wrong can cause grave problems, but the definition of wrong is multifaceted. So far we've examined the question from the critically important outward-facing perspective—what customers value and how they will respond to price changes. But for a business, even the most skillful pricing won't produce financial success if the company hasn't met the challenges of the recession on the inside. If its operations aren't competitive, if it isn't efficient, then it could still be crushed by the recession; while if it is, the recession can be a time of triumph. That's our next topic.

CHAPTER TEN

Get Fitter Faster

The right kind of operational discipline pays off powerfully in a recession

In February 2009, with the economy shrinking, unemployment rising, and stocks tanking, several holders of American Express charge cards received a letter from the company conveying an unusual offer: if you pay off your outstanding balance and close your account—that is, if you cease to be our customer—we'll send you a $300 prepaid gift card.

No credit card company had ever made an offer like that, as far as anyone in the industry could recall, yet it was probably a smart idea. As we've seen, one of this recession's most significant traits is the extraordinary amount of debt that consumers racked up even before the recession started. Credit card delinquency rates had been deteriorating for some time, but when the U.S. economy grew suddenly worse in early 2009, AmEx figured delinquencies would soon follow. With regard to certain customers—those with high balances and not much spending or payment activity—it was worth paying them to clear their debts now rather than let those debts go bad, at much higher expense to AmEx, later. Thus the unorthodox offer.

Reevaluating the economic value of customers—and of products, services, facilities, and lines of business—is one of the most important steps a company can take in tough times. That's especially so in an unusual recession like this one, when companies are more likely to encounter new challenges that demand innovative responses like American Express's. More generally, every business needs to take a fresh look at operations in a deep downturn. This isn't grand strategy. It's the nuts and bolts of business, the millions of day-to-day decisions that add up to productivity, efficiency, and financial success. In a historically severe recession, they become more important than at any other time.

Operational discipline is one of those things that all companies should pay attention to always, but most companies don't. It's easy to get lax about it in good times, and it's more fun and exciting to think about deal making and big-picture strategy. Then, when times get desperate, too many managers choose easy responses rather than smart ones, ordering across-the-board cuts or just firing people until costs come down enough. But the most successful companies think differently about operations, and in this as in all things managerial, they face a rich opportunity to leap ahead of competitors in a downturn.

The most effective moves aren't always the ones that managers reflexively make. Sometimes they're exactly the opposite. The greatest rewards go to businesses that move fastest and best in following ten practices.

▶ **Understand the new economic profitability of all your business's components.** Until you know this, you're flying blind—yet it's amazing how many companies have never known the economic profitability of their various facilities, products, services, or customers. If that's you, then there's no better time than now to learn those things for the first time. Even if you have calculated them before, it's critical to recalculate them, because the numbers may have changed significantly.

We've previously discussed economic profit, the profit that's left after deducting the correct charge for capital; it's the measure that determines the value of a business. Knowing the economic profit of the entire company is vital, but operational discipline requires knowing it in much greater detail. Companies that don't calculate it routinely must understand that other, more convenient measures are not adequate substitutes. For example, the top executives of a major retailer studied by the consultant Larry Selden believed that all their products were profitable. All products earned positive gross margins, and the executives believed they managed inventories well, so capital charges shouldn't be too great. Conclusion: nothing to worry about. But these executives ignored important costs, such as a store's operating expenses; if the shoe department occupies 10 percent of the floor space and has 10 percent of the traffic, then it should bear 10 percent of the store's costs. Just by allocating those costs properly, the company found that 25 percent of its product categories were unprofitable. Then it added capital costs, not just for inventories but also for store leases, fixtures, and other appropriate items. The result was that over 50 percent of this company's product categories were unprofitable!

Realize what this means: because the managers believed that all products were profitable, they were spending money on advertising and promotion to get people into the stores to buy items that were actually reducing the economic profit—and thus the value—of the company.

Similar analyses can be done at many levels of detail—for stores, offices, factories, even functions and processes. The analysis is often useful when applied to some entity that could be thought of as a freestanding business, something that could be sold on its own. That way, the analysis implies clear actions for fixing problems—changing the product mix, raising prices, et cetera.

Perhaps the most useful level at which to calculate economic profit is the level of individual customers or customer segments. It can be done, and many companies do it—first by learning the economic profit of different products, then by noting the product bundles purchased by different customers and allocating the costs of serving these customers. The result is a distribution of customer profitability that is remarkably similar across companies—and typically very extreme. The top 10 percent of customers generally produce profits equal to more than 100 percent of the firm's total profit, while the bottom 10 percent typically produce losses equal to about 70 percent of the firm's profit.

As with product profitability, imagine the blunders made by managers who don't know this information, and how damaging those mistakes will be in a downturn. An example is what Kmart did during the 2001 recession. With survival at stake, it launched a "super service index," a highly ambitious program of surveying customers about their satisfaction. Unfortunately, the company had no idea which customers were economically profitable and which were not, so of course it had no clue as to which kinds of customers it was satisfying. Critical questions could not be answered. Was the company delighting hordes of unprofitable customers and ticking off a smaller number of highly profitable ones? If so, its super service index score would have risen (which it did), while its stock price would have tanked (which it did). The company couldn't even begin to approach this problem. Kmart ended about the same time the recession did, filing what was then the largest retail bankruptcy petition in U.S. history.

The value of particular customers can change sharply in a recession. For example, in their attempts to reduce inventories (for reasons described in chapter 7), customers may try to shift inventory onto suppliers. A major printing company believed a certain large customer was highly profitable, but this customer required the printer to hold large inventories of expensive specialty papers; when the capital costs of all that inventory were considered, the customer wasn't profitable at all. Big customers may also demand large discounts in a recession, reducing or wiping out their profitability. If a company doesn't know this information—and doesn't recheck it frequently—it has no prayer of responding intelligently and maximizing its performance in a down economy.

Look at your world through a green lens. It may seem odd to suggest considering a green initiative during a serious recession. The conventional view is that greenness may be a luxury for a company at a time when the viability of the company itself could be threatened. A prominent consultant told me he had doubts "about the sustainability of sustainability" in the current recession. But in fact, seeing the business from an environmental perspective can be a great idea in distressed times because it can reveal cost-saving opportunities that had previously been invisible.

The most impressive example is Wal-Mart, a company where thousands of managers think all day every day about new ways to cut costs. It's in the firm's DNA. You'd think that by this point in the company's life there wouldn't be a stray penny of cost left to be eliminated. Yet Doug McMillon, the former Sam's Club chief who now runs Wal-Mart's international operations, told me that when Wal-Mart started its environmental initiative, it was "as if somebody handed us a different pair of glasses, and the whole world looked different."

The company found, for example, that by eliminating excessive packaging on its private-label toys, it could save $2.4 million a year in shipping costs, 3,800 trees, and a million barrels of oil. Wal-Mart runs a fleet of over seven thousand trucks; drivers used to let their engines idle during mandatory ten-hour breaks from driving, in order to keep the cabs warm or cool. The company installed auxiliary power units, told drivers to turn off their engines during breaks, and saved $26 million a year. Equipping stores with balers to recycle and sell plastic that used to be thrown away added $28 million to profits. The Sam's Club division got its dairy suppliers to use a redesigned milk jug that fits more efficiently into trucks, eliminating eleven thousand truck deliveries per year; the jug also happens to give the milk a longer shelf life, and it costs less.

All these savings and more turned up at the most fiercely cost-averse company anywhere, just by looking at the business from a different perspective. As McMillon said, "We thought we were efficient, but we really weren't." If that's true at Wal-Mart, it's true anywhere.

Think twice before cutting the easy expenses. We've already examined the practical arguments against reflexively cutting the spending that most companies immediately cut in a downturn— R & D, advertising, travel, entertainment, and others often categorized as SG&A (selling, general, and administrative expenses). Many of those expenses are really investments that will still pay a worthwhile return, so continuing to make them in a recession can create a competitive advantage.

Sounds good in theory, and in fact this argument is supported by empirical research into top-performing companies. These are companies that stayed in the top quartile by stock-market performance and earned standout returns on capital during the period from 1982 to 1999 or that moved into this elite group during that period, as identified by McKinsey research. During years when the economy was expanding, these companies spent less than others in their industries on SG&A and advertising, as measured against sales. But in the recession of 1990–91, these excellent performers actually spent significantly more than those that lost their market leadership— 9 percent more on advertising, 14 percent more on SG&A. As the researchers put it, "successful leaders, trading short-term profitability for long-term gain, refocused rather than cut spending."

R & D presented a similar story, with this difference: the leaders spent more than their competitors on R & D even in good times. But when the recession hit, they saw a giant opportunity to gain advantage through innovation and really heavied up on R & D, more than doubling their spending versus their competitors. The leaders moved from spending about 9 percent more than the competition during economic expansions to spending 22 percent more during the recession. Where did they get the money for all that spending? Top performers had the courage to dig much more deeply into their cash reserves than did their less successful competitors. In the recession that began in 1990, "they lowered their reserves to a level 41% below that of their former peers," say the researchers. In other words, they were tremendously confident that their moves would succeed and showed it through bold financial actions.

Their confidence was justified. Many managers complain that the stock market would punish them for spending more and cutting less than competitors during a recession, but the McKinsey research reinforces other findings that we've already seen showing the opposite. The market, on average, understands what these companies are doing and rewards them. Not only were these companies top market performers during the 1982–99 period overall, but they also outperformed competitors during and immediately after the recession. By the recession's end, companies that moved into the top performing group had earned market-to-book ratios that were 25 percent higher than those of the companies left behind. Companies that were top performers all along, and thus had achieved superior market-to-book ratios even before the recession, increased their advantage on this measure by 38 percent.

The big picture from this research is clear: the most successful companies play offense, not defense, during a recession. Poor performers focus on reducing vulnerabilities and surviving. Top performers see opportunities to build advantages when their competitors have, in effect, taken themselves out of the game.

Following their example may not be easy if you haven't prepared for it. The ability of the champions to go big during a recession depends partly on their operational discipline during the preceding years. The research shows that these are extremely efficient companies. They can spend money because they've got it, and while all companies want to run lean during a recession, the best ones are already there. Bad times are when all that discipline pays off, and managers at flabby companies are right to say that they can't suddenly start performing like Olympic athletes when the going gets tough. But that excuse will get those managers only so far. Every company, even if it's in poor condition, faces a choice about where it will cut expenses in a recession and how it will spend the money it's got. If its condition is dire, like that of some automakers, it may be forced to cut sound expenses, in which case the recession will probably just hasten its demise. But most other companies can learn much from the behavior of the top performers.

Ask, what would we do if we had to sell this business? Like going green, this is another way to see your business from a new perspective and find new opportunities to build it, reshape it, and make it more efficient. Assume you'll be selling the business to a rational, well-informed buyer, so just slashing this year's expenses to produce a one-time jump in profits won't do the job. What would you do that you aren't doing now to make the company more valuable?

A productive source of insight is the experience of the best private equity firms. Every time they buy a company for their portfolio, they want to fix it, grow it, and sell it in three to seven years. The eventual buyer could be another company in the portfolio company's industry, or another private equity firm, or the public through an IPO. Sometimes the holding period is much shorter—Carlyle, Merrill Lynch, and Clayton Dubilier & Rice sold Hertz through an IPO barely a year after buying it from Ford. Occasionally it's longer; Texas Pacific Group owned preppy retailer J. Crew for nine years before taking it public. But always the goal from day one is to sell the company at a profit.

The most immediate advantage of this model, which would benefit many companies in a deep recession, is that facing such a goal changes a manager's whole mind-set. No longer seeing a corporate future that stretches indefinitely into the future, executives realize they gain nothing by resisting change; with the exit looming, driving change is their only hope. "Everybody in the company knows you're on a sprint to do well," I was told by Tom von Krannichfeldt, brought in by Carlyle Group to run one of its portfolio companies, AZ Electronic Materials. "It's not this mind-set of working for a company that's been there for a hundred years and will continue for another hundred years."

You may not want employees all thinking the company will be sold in a few years, but you definitely do want the sense of urgency that von Krannichfeldt is describing. If you knew the company had to be improved considerably and quickly—an apt description of what needs doing in a recession—one of the things you'd probably do is:

Focus intensely on a few clear goals. Public companies often get caught up in disagreements over what to measure—earnings per share, return on equity, return on net assets. Companies owned by public equity firms serenely bypass that debate. They're managed for value, the ultimate business reality. These companies tend to be especially disciplined about how to reach their cash goals, making sure they don't destroy value in the pursuit of cash. More than most companies, they insist on identifying the handful of measurements that are most important. Many companies call them key performance indicators, or KPIs. They're particularly valuable in a recession because when things go bad according to the measures that were used in good times, managers tend to find or invent new measures that look good now and argue that those are what really count. That is evading reality, and it's fatal. You can't hope for progress without being clear and unwavering about the measurements that matter.

Thus, at AZ, Carlyle and von Krannichfeldt agreed on a set of measures that would define success and that everyone would monitor continually. They're appropriate for a specialized manufacturing company; yours would probably be different. What's important is that everyone agreed on them, so there could be no evasions. They cover all the critical areas—finances, growth, productivity, quality, safety, market position. Here's the dashboard:

Financial	Productivity
EBITDA	Lean Six Sigma savings
Cash flow	Purchasing savings
Growth	Quality
Revenue by key customer	COPQ (cost of poor quality)
Revenue from products less than three years old	Customer complaints
Revenue from strategic growth segments	On-time delivery
Year-over-year sales growth	
	Safety
Profitability	Injury rates
EBITDA as percent of sales	
Cash conversion (operating cash flow as percent of EBITDA)	Market Position
DOI (days of inventory on hand)	Market growth for key products
	Market share by key products

Many of the most successful private equity outfits use an even shorter list of measures—just five, chosen to meet the needs of a particular business. These firms find that this tactic is extremely effective in focusing everyone on the critical goals and avoiding distractions. That's exactly what all companies need to do in a bad recession.

If you had to choose five measures for everyone in your business to focus on right now, what would they be? Would most people in your company come up with the same list? If not, you may have a problem.

Make executive pay a help, not a hindrance. Many companies, especially big ones, talk a lot about aligning executive pay with performance, but the connection is often weak. They typically award stock options and restricted stock on top of already substantial pay packages, giving executives much to gain but little to lose. And in big companies, those options reflect the fortunes of the overall corporation, not the performance of the specific business that a manager is running.

A deep recession is an excellent opportunity to make the game much more serious in a way that managers will embrace because it holds the potential for significant personal gain. When managers are required to buy company stock with a meaningful amount of their own money, everything changes. That's another lesson from the private equity playbook. For example, at Dunkin' Brands, owned by Bain Capital, Carlyle, and Thomas H. Lee Partners, former CEO Jon Luther told me, "I insisted that all officers invest personally. Management has a substantial amount of their personal money in this. It makes a huge difference in the forty officers of the company when they show up for work. They have an ownership mentality rather than a corporate mentality." He says the resulting difference in behavior is clear: "There's now a very different discipline in how you spend money—if it doesn't grow the business, why would you do it?"

Another effect: people just try harder. At Genpact, an outsourcing company that had been part of General Electric and was bought by General Atlantic and Oak Hill Capital Partners, CEO Pramod Bhasin sees the difference every day: "We are owners, so you fight harder for targets, fight harder to see where else you can go, stretch yourself more"—even more, he says, than at GE, where he spent twenty-five years. The behavior he describes is exactly what all companies need in a recession.

Every company wants managers who are aligned with one another, and nothing aligns a team more strongly than heavily performance-based pay reinforced by a shared knowledge that everyone has skin in the game. The big opportunity presented by a recession is that most stock valuations are deeply depressed; if ever a company were to require that managers buy stock, this would be the moment.

Don't spread the cuts evenly. It's a strong temptation because it's easy and it seems fair, at least initially: make every department and operation cut expenses by 10 percent, or cut everybody's pay uniformly. Yet that obviously makes no sense. Some parts of the business may perform much better than others in this recession, so shouldn't they be given more resources rather than deprived of them? McKinsey reports that a major European bank cut staff after the subprime crisis hurt its U.S. operations—a uniform, across-the-board reduction. The trouble was, as the researchers report, this meant that "even an alternative-investment unit delivering 60% earnings growth had to cut back its resources, negatively impacting future growth."

Imposing uniform pay cuts leads to similar problems. Equal reductions are meant to send the message that we all have to share the pain, but your star performers may feel badly demoralized when they're rewarded with the same punishment as the poor performers who are sitting just down the hall. Differentiation is at least as important in tough times as in good ones.

Don't sacrifice cash just to improve reported earnings. We've already seen how some companies make the mistake of destroying value in order to increase cash, say by cutting R & D investments. Many companies also make what we might think of as the opposite error: depleting cash just so they can increase the accounting-mandated earnings number on their required financial statements.

In certain situations a company may face a legitimate choice of how it accounts for a particular expenditure—as an expense or as an investment, and if as an investment, then a choice of the period over which it should be capitalized. If the company calls it an expense, then reported earnings take an immediate hit, but the company's tax bill also gets reduced because of the deduction. If the company calls the outlay an investment, or decides to capitalize it over many years rather than a few, then reported earnings look better—but the company pays a higher tax bill because it gets a smaller deduction. Remember, the original outlay is the same either way; the money has actually gone out the door. The choice of what to call it determines whether a company saves cash but reports lower earnings, or sends more cash to the tax man in order to report higher earnings. At any time, but especially in a deep recession, the right choice is to conserve the cash.

Note, by the way, that this bias toward expensing for tax purposes is a cash-saving measure; it doesn't affect how you categorize outflows (as expenses or as investments) for your own evaluation purposes, as discussed in chapter 7.

Take a fresh look at offshoring. A time of greater cost pressures may seem an odd moment to ask whether offshoring still makes sense, but in fact the economics have changed drastically. The labor cost advantage of manufacturing in China or Malaysia has shrunk as wages in those countries have jumped, and now that unemployment is increasing in developed economies, the wage gap in some industries may shrink further. The price of oil, while down from its peak, is still much higher than five years ago and unlikely to fall much further, in the view of many analysts, so transportation costs may also cut into offshoring's edge. Combine all the factors, and now may be a smart time to bring manufacturing back to, or at least closer to, your home market. McKinsey found, for example, that a midrange computer server could be made for much less in Asia than in the

United States in 2003, but by 2008 the advantage in landed cost had reversed—making the machine was actually cheaper in America.

Manufacturing costs aren't the only factor in an offshoring decision. Taxes, tariffs, speed, and transition costs can make a big difference. But at a time when costs count more than ever, don't assume that offshoring is still your best option.

Ask the employees where the opportunities are. In a deep downturn companies want to find every possible operational improvement, the little things that add up to big savings. The difficulty is that they could be hiding in a million places. Staples, the giant retailer of office products, reported that in the midst of this recession it had found $21 million of efficiencies in the way it runs its warehouses. Finding such substantial savings seemed remarkable considering that Staples is widely regarded as a very tight ship that is always taking out unnecessary costs. I asked the chief financial officer, Christine Komola, how they knew where to look for the savings. She replied immediately, "Ask the associates. They know."

Headquarters is always ordering cost cuts, but headquarters often doesn't know where the greatest potential savings are lurking. Somebody knows, however, and in a downturn it's vital that everyone be asked.

Operational excellence isn't every company's strength. An excellent book, *The Discipline of Market Leaders,* even argued that it shouldn't be—that every company needs to focus on just one of three possible strengths (the other two are product leadership and customer intimacy). But in a deep recession, when every dollar of profit becomes far harder to earn, the value of operational excellence multiplies, and every company needs to get better at it.

The truth is that in operations and every other aspect of running a business, the stakes become much higher in a recession. Because room for error is so drastically constricted, every decision carries a greater potential for damage or even disaster. As a result, everyone becomes far more conscious of risk. Thinking properly about risk thus becomes one of the critical skills for every manager in a recession, and especially in this recession, which was caused in part by staggeringly poor misreading of risks. Understanding risk in the new environment is therefore our next topic.

CHAPTER ELEVEN

Understand All Your Risks

*Seize this moment to take a broader view of what might
go wrong in your business*

J ust a few weeks before the subprime crisis exploded in the United
States and pushed the economy down the slope that would lead to
recession within six months, a risk consulting firm called Protiviti
published its annual Risk Barometer. The report detailed the results of
a survey that questioned 150 top-level executives in U.S. companies.
The executives were asked, among many other questions, "How effectively does your company identify and manage all potentially
significant risks?" The answers were then sorted by the respondents'
industries.

In retrospect, maybe the results shouldn't surprise us. Respondents to this question seemed appropriately humble in all industries
except two: financial services and real estate. Of the executives in
these, the two industries that were about to go over the precipice of
a once-in-a-lifetime disaster, 72 percent gave themselves the highest
possible score. No other industries came anywhere near this level
of confidence in their own preparedness for whatever fate might
throw at them.

But that wasn't the only way in which those executives deluded themselves. They were asked also about their "risk appetite," and by that measure the financial services and real estate respondents were much more modest; they did not rate themselves highest. Executives in health care and life sciences considered themselves willing to take on considerably more risk.

Looking at that combination of results, the researchers concluded that one grouping of companies was clearly better prepared for the risks of the future than any of the others, and that was financial services and real estate companies: "these organizations not only possess a reduced risk appetite, but also a very high level of effectiveness at identifying and managing all potentially significant risks," the report stated. "This suggests a much better position relative to the other sector groupings." Of course, these companies were precisely the ones that were within weeks of getting walloped by the greatest calamity most of them had ever encountered, which would destroy several of them.

Here we see all of the largest issues in trying to manage the risks facing your business: why it's important, why it's so hard, why you have to keep doing it anyway. If it seems ironic that the worst-hit industries in this recession were the ones most confident in their readiness for risk, it really shouldn't. In fact, how could it be otherwise? Only a company that's very sure of its place in the universe could fail to notice the Texas-sized asteroid hurtling toward it. That's part of what makes risk management so mind-bending: the most dangerous risk you face is by definition the one you can't even conceive of. Once you've thought of it, you can prepare for it—and your biggest risk becomes something else that has never crossed your mind. In the survey mentioned above, most executives thought the largest risk they faced was what a competitor might do. The possibility that the world financial system might seize up and this might be the largest risk facing every company, regardless of industry, was beyond imagining for most people.

That's why this recession presents such a rich opportunity for

companies to improve the way they manage risk: we've been shown—
and not just told—that we must all think about risk far more expan-
sively than we do. Around the world, thousands of companies were
analyzing their risks diligently, and plenty of them (not just in finance
and real estate) believed they were well prepared. They just never
considered the type of cascading systemic failure that actually
occurred. Of course, now we'll all be preparing for that type of
catastrophe—which means the greatest risk we face is something
new that we haven't imagined.

Seeing the Risk You Never Imagined

Thus, now is the moment when every company is most strongly
motivated to get serious about managing risk, and that would be a
good thing even if this recession hadn't happened. Well before it
started, large trends were making the world economy much crazier,
faster changing, and riskier than it used to be. Look at Standard &
Poor's ratings of equity risks, gauging a company's ability to deliver
steady earnings, which range from A+ for the least risky companies
to D for bankrupt ones. (These ratings aren't to be confused with the
much-maligned debt ratings, which became notoriously generous
when applied to complex structured securities prerecession; the equity ratings have a much longer pedigree and have remained strict.)
In 1985 about 41 percent of companies earned the least risky ratings,
while just 35 percent were in the high-risk grouping, according to an
analysis by Mercer Management Consulting. By the end of 2008 the
picture had reversed dramatically; only 12 percent were highly rated,
and 74 percent were high risk. That's what economists call a secular
shift—a big, broad increase in uncertainty and volatility across the
economy.

How should companies respond to the world's increasing riski-
ness? Some moves are predictable, though not necessarily helpful.

In the early days of the crisis, companies were stampeding to appoint chief risk officers, though this often had the feel of slamming the barn door after the horses were long gone; Citigroup, JPMorgan Chase, Merrill Lynch, and Morgan Stanley all named CROs after the meltdown was well under way. Creating such a position can be effective if the CEO wants it to be, though some companies believe they get greater accountability by assigning responsibility for specific risks to particular managers.

Also suddenly fashionable is creating a risk committee within the board of directors; UBS did so after writing off some $40 billion of bad investments, for example, another instance of the barn-door phenomenon. Many of these new committees seem to have been launched for the sake of appearances, since obviously boards have always carried ultimate responsibility for monitoring risks to the enterprise. In any case, it's far from clear that stand-alone risk committees are effective. Bear Stearns had one. In the UK, so did the failed bank Northern Rock.

More important than structure is how companies actually behave with respect to risk. The enormously destructive power of this recession teaches five lessons that every company can apply for much better understanding and control of its risks.

Turbocharge your imagination. Because the events that do the worst damage are the ones you never conceived of, effective risk management begins with an eternal quest to imagine possibilities you hadn't even thought about before.

That's difficult not only because it requires you to stretch your mind in new ways but also because the most valuable thoughts you develop will be—by definition—the ones that cause your colleagues to doubt your judgment, the seemingly bizarre and even ridiculous possibilities that are not on any conventional list of dangers. When executives received that 2007 risk survey described earlier, the greatest danger they faced—a global financial system meltdown—wasn't even offered as one of the choices. Part of your job is to make sure that the biggest risks your business actually faces are at least on the list of possibilities.

The present moment is a great time to reimagine the dangers you might face, for two reasons. First, the scale of the global recession is so great that it reminds us all just how pinched and puny our imaginations had become. Because the United States had not seen a serious recession in twenty-five years, it was extremely difficult in the booming days from 2002 through 2007 to liberate our minds and picture events that would go off the charts into territory we hadn't seen in many decades. The possibility of what actually happened seemed genuinely outlandish back then, and even to mention it inside a company was to sound like a nut. Now, for the first time in a long while, it's safe to raise any possibility. We've all been reminded that truly anything can happen. The cultural challenge inside organizations will be to maintain that spirit of openness.

The second reason this is such an excellent time to reimagine risks is that we can now look back and identify the voices that were in fact envisioning this crisis before it happened. Imagining outlandish possibilities is hard, but fortunately we don't have to do it alone. Plenty of others are always doing it as well, and our present situation is a powerful reminder that those scorned, lonely voices are worth our attention.

That doesn't mean listening to the loonies, who are always with us and who will even be right every so often. Rather, it means listening to respectable thinkers who are fighting the tide of conventional wisdom, of whom there were plenty during the boom years. As mentioned previously, Professor Robert Shiller of Yale, using extensive, rigorous research, told the world for years that U.S. home prices were insanely high and would have to fall by at least 30 percent to return to normal, and would inevitably do so—but his prediction was so extreme and frightening that most people ignored it. The successful fund manager Jeremy Grantham declared flatly that global asset prices had formed a bubble that had to burst, but of course no one wanted to hear that. Ditto with the warnings of Professor Nouriel Roubini of New York University, who during the good years made unhedged predictions of a massive, real-estate-triggered recession. Even the *McKinsey Quarterly*—not exactly a journal of wild-eyed extremism—described the financial system's growing dangers in a stunningly prescient 2004 article on credit derivatives. The risk, it said, was that "some players—among them insurance companies and commercial banks—are pushing too aggressively into the market, distorting prices and raising the possibility that one company's large, unexpected losses could upset the entire system." That sentence does everything except actually mention the name AIG to describe what developed. The article foresaw other dangers quite specifically: "the growing use of credit derivatives is transferring risk on an increasingly large scale in ways that are mostly opaque to investors and regulators." It said bluntly that many firms "are taking on too much risk in the credit derivatives market without fully understanding their exposure" and that investors must understand "the way correlations among individual credit risks can significantly influence a portfolio's overall risk profile." Exactly how the system would actually blow up was laid out in clear prose for anyone who cared to read it.

The point is not that we all should have realized that those particular prognosticators would be right. No one can know that. Rather, the point is that those viewpoints were available. We don't always have to imagine the unimaginable on our own, because it is often being imagined for us by credible thinkers. What we have to do—but not many did—is open our minds to the possibility that they could be right.

An important element of contemplating the unimaginable is knowing that it's never just one event. It's always a sequence that unfolds in truly unexpected ways. An apt example is what happened to the World Trade Center on September 11. The idea that a passenger jet might crash into one of the towers had been thought of; it was a fairly obvious possibility, especially considering that a plane had once crashed into the Empire State Building. So the towers were designed quite deliberately to withstand that impact, and they did so; the initial impacts from the planes didn't knock either tower down. What no one imagined was this possible sequence: a large plane with a nearly full fuel tank hits a tower; the impact jars the fireproofing from the steel girders that support the building; the enormous quantity of jet fuel ignites and creates extraordinarily high temperatures in the structure; the steel girders soften and bend; the structure above the fire lists to one side, creating stresses that the structure below was never designed to support; the tower collapses. In theory, that sequence could have been imagined. In reality, it wasn't.

Imagining sequences that have never previously occurred is so difficult that even the greatest geniuses fail at it. That was the lesson of the hedge fund Long-Term Capital Management, whose founders included two Nobel Prize–winning economists. They believed the only thing that could wipe them out was a "ten-sigma event," which in statistics means an event so rare it could be expected to occur once in the history of the universe. In fact it occurred about four years after LTCM was founded—a combination of unexpected divergences in certain interest rates, plus Russia's devaluation of the ruble and other factors. In retrospect, that sequence doesn't seem so mind-bogglingly hard to imagine, but failure to imagine it cost LTCM's investors billions.

Build scenarios. Cold-war military strategists originated scenario planning, so by now the technique is well developed. Properly guided, it can help managers see important possible events they wouldn't have imagined, because it's all about thinking through possible sequences. The best and most famous example is how the technique helped Shell respond to the Arab oil embargo of the 1970s. It's important to emphasize that no scenario told Shell's managers the embargo would happen; this is a strategic planning technique, not Nostradamus. But one of the scenarios developed by the strategy group envisioned an accident in Saudi Arabia that raised the price of oil, causing Arab producers to rethink why they set prices as they did. Shell managers extended the possible sequence further and realized that Arab producers, angry with the United States for its support of Israel in the Six-Day War, might believe they could serve many purposes at once by launching an embargo or restricting supply.

To repeat, nothing in the exercise told Shell managers to expect an embargo. But because they had thought through possible sequences, they could see how events might be leading to an embargo, and when it happened they were much better prepared than any competitors to respond. The common view in the industry is that Shell came through the oil shock far better than any other major producer.

Shell's scenarios continue to do their job well, and while they're intended to help a global energy company, they're widely applicable. (An extensive outline of the firm's current scenarios is available at www. shell.com/scenarios.) The scenarios in use when the global financial crisis began envisioned a world shaped by three large forces: a demand for efficiency and corporate performance as capitalism spreads and capital markets become global, a demand for community as developing nations seek a more peaceful future, and a demand for security as the world seemingly becomes more dangerous. The scenario developers realized that those forces would inevitably conflict, and so they worked through possible sequences of what might happen when they did. Nothing in the scenarios predicted a worldwide recession, but they encouraged the developers to think about a world in which "disruption of both international security and trust in the marketplace highlight the importance of the role of the state." That's a pretty good description of the world we are now entering.

Another set of deeply developed scenarios that will stimulate your mind comes from the U.S. National Intelligence Council (www. cia.gov/nic), picturing five possible futures for 2020. Will globalization advance peacefully and prosperously—with China and India becoming economic superpowers? Or will the United States continue to dominate the new global order? Or will spreading nuclear weapons lead to a world so secure it's Orwellian? Your company's future is no more than two steps removed from the answers to those questions.

Scenario planning is sometimes criticized because it's only as good as the people doing it. Quite right. But that fact shouldn't discourage any organization from using the technique. Partly that's because thoroughly developed scenarios such as those mentioned are publicly available and provide excellent launch points for your own thinking. In addition, the mere act of going through the exercise is guaranteed to expand your thinking about your organization's possible futures, which is always worthwhile.

Think in probabilities while realizing their limitations. If you can imagine an event, you can try to assign a probability to it, either in absolute terms—0.1 percent, 3 percent, 50 percent—or at least relative to other events. That sounds obvious and easy, but it's excruciatingly difficult in practice because our brains aren't wired that way. Nassim Nicholas Taleb in his book *Fooled by Randomness* cites an example: ask a sample of travelers at an airport how much they'd pay for an insurance policy that would give their beneficiary one million dollars if they die from any cause on their trip. Then ask another sample how much they'd pay for a policy that would pay one million dollars if they're killed by terrorists on their trip. People will pay more for the second policy, though that clearly makes no sense. We just do not think rationally about probabilities, a tendency every manager must fight.

The strength of thinking in probabilities is that it forces us to bring to the surface and confront thoughts that we may not realize we're carrying around. It enables us to avoid the mistake described by Taleb, for example. More broadly, it leads us to act more rationally. In the current environment, for example, the possibility of a major competitor failing in the next twelve months may have crossed your mind. If you then ask yourself how likely you believe that to be, you may realize you have no clear view, in which case you'll want to gather much more information about such a significant possibility and form a probability estimate. Or you may realize that you actually do have a clear view and consider the probability about 40 percent—but then realize that you haven't prepared nearly enough for a possibility that you consider so likely. Either way, focusing on probability has made you better off.

The limitation of thinking probabilistically is that probabilities are meaningful only for events with some kind of history. For flipping coins and rolling dice, probabilities are highly precise. The concept still has meaning for the chances of a competitor failing, since companies are constantly failing even though circumstances are always unique. For an event as unusual as the current recession, trying to assign a probability beforehand may not be a meaningful exercise. But evaluating the chances of events that are affected by the recession— such as changes in your company's earnings, changes in prices of inputs, changes in behaviors of competitors or customers—is most definitely worth doing.

Use the power of markets. Prediction markets, in which real people bet real money on the likelihood of specific events, have been around for years and attracted lots of acclaim after correctly predicting the squeaker 2004 U.S. presidential election. They have also been remarkably successful at predicting many other events, from the outcomes of football matches to the winners of Academy Awards. Of course they aren't always right, especially when predicting events in the distant future, but at any given moment they are likely to be at least as accurate as any other type of prediction.

One reason these markets are so valuable to companies trying to manage risk is that the markets now set prices on a very wide array of possible events that may matter to your business. When Microsoft will release the next version of its operating system, which countries will adopt or drop the euro as their currency, whether a particular cold fusion experiment will be replicated—all of these possibilities and a great many more are being priced every day in online prediction markets, with the price showing the market's shifting view of the probabilities.

Another way you can harness the power of these markets is by creating them among your own employees, generally with small amounts of money furnished by the company, focused on exactly the questions you want answered. Hewlett-Packard has found that internal prediction markets are able to forecast sales more accurately than the marketing manager could. Eli Lilly has used them to predict the success of drug research with uncanny accuracy. Well-designed prediction markets can give managers new insight into specific risks and how they would affect the company.

Create an organization and culture that adapts quickly to new realities. A tall order, admittedly. But much of the recent thinking on corporate risk assumes that in an increasingly volatile and fast-changing world, a great many events simply cannot be prepared for. Try though you might to imagine possible futures, you can never entirely succeed. To the extent that you don't, the key then becomes responding quickly and effectively to the bolt from the blue, and the number one impediment—incredible yet obvious—is failing to accept that the trouble has happened. In New Orleans, immediately after Hurricane Katrina passed through, people were dancing in Bourbon Street; once the wind had stopped blowing, they thought everything would be okay.

A tendency to avoid reality, to minimize bad news, may lie deep in a corporate culture. But while most cultural change must start at the top, this change can start anywhere. This recession is an unprecedented opportunity to begin such a change.

Beyond the importance of culture, a company's organizational form can give it an advantage in responding to unanticipated risks. Some managers have decided that a radically changed business world calls for a radically organized company. The most extreme example of meeting chaos with chaos is probably Semco, the celebrated Brazilian outfit where there are virtually no job titles, a few executives trade the CEO role every six months, and workers set their own hours and choose their managers by vote. I once asked Semco's CEO and principal owner, Ricardo Semler, if this was all an expression of some kind of social idealism. "It's not about values," he said, speaking as vehemently as I'd ever heard him. "It's about competitive advantage."

Maybe your firm can't be run like Semco (though exactly why not?), but decentralization and an anticontrol ethos seem to characterize a growing number of companies that adapt and succeed in this high-risk environment. No one at W. L. Gore has a job title, to take an example from *Fortune* magazine's ranking of America's one hundred best companies to work for, which on average far outperform other companies. Another: any employee of Whole Foods Market can look up anyone else's salary. Conventional wisdom says such policies would create chaos, yet in a fast-changing world they seem to have the opposite effect.

Google's let-a-thousand-flowers-bloom approach to strategy is similar in spirit. With umpteen new business initiatives being worked on at any given moment, you might suppose the place would collapse in disorder. But Google's top executives know that the greatest risk they face is a future challenge to the company's gold-mine paid-search advertising business. While constantly pruning ventures that don't work, such as their businesses that sold radio and newspaper advertising, they continue to let employees pursue their own new ideas, knowing that one of them could someday save the company.

Nor is that approach to strategy as radical as it seems. Former Shell executive Arie de Geus studied the world's longest-lived companies and concluded that something like Google's philosophy was critical. Surviving unanticipated risks was all about "letting things happen in the margin: allowing activities . . . to be set up by not coming down like a ton of bricks on every diversion in which local people seem to believe fervently." When the core business gets whacked, as it always does, something else is there. But managers must maintain years of faith that a degree of letting go will pay off.

Letting go of control is almost impossibly painful for many managers, yet an even more profound problem becomes important when companies must make large changes frequently, as they do now. It's letting go of the past. Peter Drucker identified the key management challenge of the twenty-first century as leading change, and he believed the most important policy for doing that was "to abandon yesterday." By *yesterday* he meant whatever no longer works—a strategy, a business model, a form of organization, a product line. Yet abandoning yesterday is excruciatingly difficult. Yesterday is known, it's comfortable, and the fact that it used to work inspires hope that it will work again. By contrast, trying anything new will always produce problems. So companies nurture yesterday far too long. What's especially insidious, Drucker observed, is that "to maintain yesterday is always difficult and extremely time-consuming" and "therefore always commits the institution's scarcest and most valuable resources—and above all, its ablest people—to nonresults." Which means they're not available where most needed, to create tomorrow.

Of course, the situation isn't hopeless; companies do manage this critical job. In a historically brave move decades ago, Intel completely bailed out of dynamic random access memory, the product on which it had built its entire early success. The company now known as Thomson Reuters abandoned newspapers, which had made it successful and famous, reasoning that newspapers were the past in the digital age. General Electric has a reputation for being extraordinarily disciplined about such decisions, yet it's still making major appliances in Louisville, where it hasn't earned a dime of profit in years and has no prospect of doing so. By the time GE decided to put that business up for sale, the current recession had taken hold and buyers were scarce. Logic had said to abandon the business or the location long ago, yet in this case even GE had a hard time saying good-bye.

Thinking deeply about risk is a way of thinking about your company at the highest level, since it forces you to consider the future viability of everything, ranging from operational details to strategy and culture. The great opportunity of this recession is the chance not only to rethink your company's risks, but also to rethink its risk-management practices and make them much better. Your organization may never be more motivated to do those things than it is today. That's one of the many opportunities to strengthen your business that this recession presents, as we've seen over the past several chapters. Now, having followed those opportunities all the way through to those that will improve your business at the highest level, we must turn to a different type of opportunity inherent in this recession—the opportunity to strengthen yourself.

CHAPTER TWELVE

Don't Forget to Grow Yourself

Why this downturn is a unique opportunity for self-development

The recession that followed World War II was hard on everybody, but it was especially tough for Bill Hewlett and Dave Packard. Supplying equipment to the government had been a big part of their young company's business, and of course that revenue mostly disappeared when the war ended. Beyond that problem, the overall economic contraction that followed the clifflike drop in government spending meant that companies—HP's other class of customers, since it didn't then sell to consumers—weren't buying either. The founders had realized that the war's end would bring a slowdown, but they had never anticipated how bad it would be. The firm faced a crisis of survival.

It was one of those moments when the behavior of a company's leaders in a brief period will determine its future for a very long time. Hewlett and Packard had built their business from the beginning on the principles of loyalty and trust, but in these circumstances they realized that they simply could not avoid mass layoffs. They fired 60 percent of their employees. Many corporate leaders have felt forced to do the same, but they haven't all been affected in the same way. Hewlett and Packard were so traumatized by the experience that they resolved never to let it happen again, and in their thirty remaining years of running the company, they never did. As their biographer Michael S. Malone has reported, "HP was actually willing to forgo extra hiring during good times, thus risking the loss of added revenues, to keep from having to mass fire employees during the bad."

The recession trauma thus changed the company, and it also changed the people. Those who remained after the layoff were forced to stretch themselves in new ways. The company's manufacturing chief turned himself into a knockout marketer and was so successful that he remained in that role for the rest of his career. Even Packard himself found muscles that no one suspected he had. Though never considered a genius engineer—that was Bill Hewlett's role—Packard returned to the lab at this time when the company was desperate for new products, and he invented one. It was a voltmeter, the beginning of a product line that would serve the company quite profitably for fifty years. Packard never invented any more products; his genius was managing the company. But when a dire situation pushed him beyond his apparent abilities, he found the strength to go there.

We've all had the experience of facing situations much worse than any we've ever encountered. They can be emergencies or accidents, or a loved one facing serious illness, or the prospect of financial ruin. Such calamities visit everyone eventually. In the worst case, they damage us and leave us weaker, diminished. In the best case they change us permanently into stronger people. Which of those two possible effects actually happens will shape the course of our whole lives, and the good news is that it's much more within our control than we tend to think. Obviously, many things are outside our control, and if our luck is bad enough then we are cooked. But in the vast majority of bad-news scenarios, like the one facing the Hewlett-Packard company and its people after World War II, what determines whether we are damaged or strengthened is how we respond.

This recession is much worse than the one following World War II, and for millions of people worldwide it's a time of deep personal trials of many types. Business leaders are forced to fire people after years of trying to build an employee-centered culture. The unemployed can't support their families and may find themselves competing with friends for new jobs. At just the worst time, people's most important assets, their homes and investment nest eggs, are worth a fraction of what they were, and that's not counting the losses suffered by victims of a truly astounding number of investment scams being revealed around the world. Truly everyone is being stress tested.

In previous chapters we've investigated the wide range of business opportunities to be found in a deep recession. In addition to each of those, the most valuable opportunities of all for many businesspeople—for their companies and above all for themselves— are the opportunities for personal growth. We can find them at three levels, all of which are apparent in the experience of Bill Hewlett and Dave Packard after World War II. At one level is the development of leadership; successful leaders reliably do a certain few things in a crisis, including confronting the unvarnished truth, as the HP founders did in their worst corporate crisis up to that point. At another level is more specific personal development in any realm. Whether it's engineering, marketing, or anything else, the new demands of a deep recession turn out to be exactly the right prescription for making us better—or at least they can be if properly understood. At the third level is what we might call the personal growth of the organization, the development of its culture. Out of the crucible of the postwar recession came a key element of HP's culture, the idea that everyone from the top down would always be working to make mass layoffs unnecessary. That ethos helped make HP one of America's greatest places to work and one of its most successful organizations of any kind for many decades.

A crisis can spark growth in these three ways, and we'll examine each of them in turn. But the growth isn't automatic. Plenty of organizations and people have been destroyed by crisis. Which outcome we reach is mostly up to us.

Using Crisis to Become a Better Leader

Crisis is the ultimate leadership opportunity, but not every leader rises to the challenge. For every inspiring story of James Burke and the Tylenol crisis, there's at least one less heralded tale of a leader who blows it. Coca-Cola CEO Douglas Ivester happened to be in Paris in July 1999, when news reports said that cans of bad Coke had made several Belgian schoolchildren sick—a major crisis for one of the world's most valuable brands. Ivester, a brilliant financial executive with a sharply analytical mind, quickly determined that all production procedures were being followed and that his products did not pose any health risks. He assumed these facts would carry the day, so he got on his plane and flew back to Atlanta. But more people got sick, images of suffering children dominated TV news, politicians demanded action, and the mess eventually cost Coke hundreds of millions of dollars plus years of distrust and bad will from all its stakeholders. It also contributed to Ivester's getting fired within months. In a crisis, he turned out to be a manager, not a leader.

A crisis like this recession demands five actions of a leader. They're simple to state and may seem simple to do, but they aren't. Finding the strength to do them will contribute significantly to any leader's growth.

Stand up and be seen. This most basic requirement is important for a fundamental reason that is often forgotten: people want to be led. That's worth emphasizing in an era when many organizations are trying to flatten their structures, and hierarchy is often regarded as bad. Lots of organizations do need to be flattened, but that doesn't contradict the hunger for leadership that all people feel in times like these.

The reasons are deep. We want the leader to be a repository for our fears. When people are desperately worried, they want to know that someone with greater power than theirs is working to solve their problems. It makes sleeping at night a little easier. People also want the leader to speak for them, to fulfill their deep need to give voice to their anxieties. The leader commands a larger stage and can meet that need in a more satisfying way than can most people individually. And people want to be led because they understand that no group accomplishes much of anything without a leader. Most of us have been thrown into group situations with no designated leader, yet a leader always emerges because everyone knows it must be so.

Thus, successful leaders in a crisis first make emphatically clear that they are present and on the job. Remember how much of Rudolph Giuliani's effectiveness after the September 11 attacks resulted merely from his visibility. He didn't have many answers. But on the day itself he visited Ground Zero six times and gave three press conferences, and in the following days he seemed not to sleep. Remember also how President Bush was criticized for flying from Florida, where he was that morning, to an Air Force base in Louisiana rather than directly back to Washington. There were sound security reasons for what he did, and his detour lasted only a few hours, but Americans wanted him visible and on the scene.

This kind of visibility isn't easy, because the leader in a crisis has a million things to do, most of which require being on the phone or meeting with small groups. In a business crisis, lawyers may be advising the leader not to make any public statements. Yet it must be done.

Michael Dell's company was not large or well established in the early 1990s when he was scheduled to appear at a conference where I was moderating. The day before, his company had announced unexpectedly terrible results. The stock had plunged, and some people wondered whether Dell himself, who wasn't yet thirty, could lead his organization past this. The situation was so serious that most of us at the conference assumed he wouldn't show up. But he did, appearing unfazed and explaining his plan. Simply appearing reassured his constituencies and increased their confidence for the future.

Be calm and in control. People assume that the leader knows more about the crisis than they do and thus look to him or her for cues about how serious it is. The result is a clear example of a self-fulfilling prophecy. Franklin Roosevelt, who famously realized the nation had nothing to fear but fear itself, knew what he was doing in keeping his cigarette holder tilted jauntily upward during public appearances. Ronald Heifetz, a leadership authority at Harvard's Kennedy School of Government, has said that "[During a crisis, a leader's] first mechanism to contain distress must be to contain himself. If [a leader] remains poised and indicates through his calm demeanor that the situation is serious but that there is no cause for a panic, he reduces the possibility of one."

Behaving that way isn't easy because you may have excellent reasons for not feeling calm at all. Giuliani's self-possession immediately after September 11 was widely regarded as another key element of his effectiveness, yet he always realized that the chance of new attacks was unknowable and possibly great. His demeanor was all the more critical as a result.

Be decisive. It's amazing how people who would be at one another's throats in good times will accept that in a crisis, decisions have to be made. At moments when it's most important that action be agreed upon, circumstances will often conspire to make that possible. Treasury Secretary Henry Paulson told the leaders of Congress in the autumn of 2008 that he needed $700 billion authorized to prevent financial catastrophe, and they agreed almost immediately;

getting enough other legislators on board took several days, but it all happened faster than would have been conceivable otherwise. Similarly, when Paulson called the chiefs of America's largest banks into a conference room and told them how much of their equity the federal government intended to buy and on what terms, they all agreed on the spot. Whether Paulson made the right decisions has been debated ever since, and that fact underscores the point: the debate happened afterward, not before. Leaders in a crisis must not lose their rare opportunity to act.

The difficulty is that just when decisions are most easily accepted, they're hardest to make. All business decisions are made with incomplete information, and that's especially true in the heat of a crisis. At the same time, the stakes are much higher than usual. Every instinct tells you to decide more slowly than usual, yet it's vital that you decide more quickly.

Show fearlessness. When Robert the Bruce led the Scots against the English at the Battle of Bannockburn, he led them literally, riding a horse in front of the rest. A mounted English knight spotted him, lowered his lance, and charged. Bruce stopped and didn't move as the knight thundered toward him. Then, at the last moment, he stood in his stirrups, turned sideways, swung his battle-ax, and split the passing knight's helmet (and head) in two. Bruce's troops were so inspired that they roared into battle and won the greatest victory in the history of their nation.

We no longer think it wise to put our military leaders in the first wave of an attack, but the principle remains. We want our leaders to show us that they're not afraid. In business that means facing bad news head on without cringing. The effective leader announces trouble in unvarnished terms—people can smell evasion a mile away—then explains confidently how it will be defeated. Fearlessness can be shown more tangibly as well, when a leader cuts his own pay or, even more powerfully, uses his own money to buy company stock, as several CEOs have done in this recession.

Note that the advice here is "show fearlessness," not "be fearless." A prominent CEO who didn't want to be quoted for obvious reasons told me, "Any CEO who isn't terrified in this recession has no sense at all." To suggest that you be fearless would be ridiculous. But what counts is what you show. Robert the Bruce was probably terrified. It didn't matter.

Explain the crisis in a larger context. Extensive research has shown that how people are affected by stress depends heavily on how they see it. Those who see stressful events as bad, abnormal, and inescapable tend to suffer from them much more seriously than do people who see those same events as normal, interesting elements of life from which they can learn and to which they can respond. Some research has found that members of the first group suffer much worse health than those in the second group. The first group burns out more quickly and performs much worse than the second group. Yet in the research, both groups are subjected to the same stress. The difference is in how they regard it.

This recession is enormously stressful for millions of people, so how they choose to respond within themselves becomes extremely important. A critical question for leaders is whether they can help everyone in the organization respond more like members of the second group. The answer seems to be yes.

The challenge consists of giving shape to events that have occurred and are occurring, portraying them as interesting, normal elements of life that may be no fun but that we can deal with while learning and growing. When the stock market was dropping in late 2008, I asked Charles Schwab about it. He began his answer by saying, "I've been through nine of these darn breaks. This happens to be the most pervasive in terms of how it has spread through the economy." He went on to explain how it differed from previous market declines and how the market would eventually climb back up. This was precisely a group-two response, starting with the idea that what some investors considered financial Armageddon was really just part of a very long pattern. His overall message was that this is interesting and something to which we're all capable of responding.

Thus, the way a leader makes sense of events and gives meaning to them is revealed as one of his or her most important jobs in a crisis. Much of the research in this area has focused on the military, where stress is most extreme and the stakes are highest. Colonel Paul T. Bartone of National Defense University, after extensive research on this topic, has concluded that leaders really can shape the meaning of events for others in ways that help them respond better: "By the policies and priorities they establish, the directives they give, the advice and counsel they offer, the stories they tell, and perhaps most important the examples they provide, leaders may indeed alter the manner in which their subordinates interpret and make sense of their experiences," he has written. Such leaders "encourage others to interpret stressful events as interesting challenges that they are capable of meeting, and in any case can learn and benefit from."

It's clear that each of these five behaviors is in fact highly effective at all times, not just in a crisis. It's also clear that each one is difficult. The great opportunity of this recession is that it has created the most intense and demanding environment for developing these abilities that most managers have ever experienced. The most successful are seeing the recession in that light and are seizing the opportunity to become much more effective leaders for the rest of their lives—a classic group-two response, by the way.

Now Is the Time to Build All Abilities

Because a recession demands so much more of leaders, it offers them an opportunity to build their skills to much higher levels. But of course a downturn also demands more of practically everyone in virtually every part of their lives. So we all face more and richer opportunities to grow than we do in normal times. In fact, these opportunities are even greater than most people realize.

The reason is connected to the way people get better at anything they do. Research has established that what turns average performers into great performers is a process of being continually pushed just beyond their current abilities and then responding to the new challenges with focused efforts to overcome them, accompanied by abundant feedback about the results. Following that process over time seems to be the one trait that characterizes great performers in every field. The process is simple to describe and sounds straightforward, but in reality few people pursue it for any significant period. Partly that's because it's hard; constantly reaching just beyond what you're able to do is effortful and even painful by definition, and plenty of people just won't want to do that.

But a more important reason that most people don't follow this well-defined path to better performance is that most work settings actually discourage them from doing it. Constantly attempting what you can't quite do, which is the essence of the process, is a recipe for trouble in most jobs. It means that you will inevitably make mistakes and have failures. Now, if you ask accomplished businesspeople, as I have often done, whether they learned more from their successes or their failures, 100 percent of them will say the latter. But most employers don't want to hear that your mistakes have been an absolutely necessary part of your growth. They just want you to perform. So that's what most people do in their jobs, operating entirely within their comfort zones and, as a result, not getting any better. We know this not just from observing it in our own workplaces but also from considerable research showing that most people improve rapidly in the early days of a given job, then plateau and may continue for years thereafter without progressing.

It must be noted that a few companies don't fit this pattern of discouraging progress. The great management academies such as Procter & Gamble, General Electric, Hindustan Unilever, and McKinsey are always trying to develop people by moving them into jobs that stretch their abilities. But even these companies cannot stretch every employee's abilities every day, and of course most people work for employers that are less enlightened than these. So everyone faces an opportunity to extend their skills, if only they will take it.

Seen against this backdrop, the precise nature of the recession opportunity is clear. It pushes each of us past our current abilities without our having to take any special steps at all. The question is then how we will respond to being shoved outside our comfort zones. One option is to evade the new challenge, trying to narrow our work responsibilities and retreating into what we already know. The other option is to make focused efforts to meet the new challenge, following the established process that leads to great performance.

The most successful companies and people are already following the second course in this recession. For example, a consumer packaged goods company decided to reach for a goal that many would consider foolhardy at any time, let alone in a severe recession: persuading Wal-Mart to pay a higher price for some of its products. To pursue this audacious goal, the company first focused on the problem's details, specifying all the reasons the price rise was justified and good for both parties. It taught this material to the appropriate salespeople. It schooled them also in the objections that Wal-Mart's buyers were likely to raise, and in the best responses. Then the company videotaped the salespeople in mock meetings with the buyers, providing feedback in the form of critiques from a consultant plus the deeply powerful tapes themselves. It reiterated these steps until the salespeople had mastered their new skills. The whole process followed exactly the routine that all great performers use. It entailed far more work than salespeople at this company (or most companies) were used to, but that's the price of superior performance. And it worked—the company got its price increases.

Another company, a medical products firm, used a similar approach when it decided to increase sales of a particular product in this recession, but it added a clever extra element to the process. The product was specialized and complex, so the salespeople required extensive training in how it worked, how it was used, and how to sell it to doctors and hospitals. Rather than just asking salespeople to learn all that material, the company asked them to learn it and then prepare themselves to teach it. The sales team prepared, practiced, and revised their presentations over a six-week period, receiving hours of feedback and coaching from managers. As a result, they mastered the material far more completely than ever before. The company also trained the sales team in use of the product, using medical simulation devices, again in keeping with the principles of great performance—pushing past existing skills with focused effort, repetition, and feedback. And the company used videotaping, much as the consumer packaged goods company did.

The results, as a company executive explained to me, were "astounding." Sales growth for the product increased from 1.5 percent annually prerecession to 10.5 percent during the recession. About 25 percent of customers who tried the product converted to it before the recession. After the improvement of the sales team's skills—and during the recession year of 2008—95 percent of customers converted. Again, it wasn't easy. An executive told me "there was significant pushback" from the salespeople regarding the time and work required, which was significantly more than they were used to. Yet consider what happened: by improving its salespeople's skills through a well-understood process, this company actually increased its sales and profits by several million dollars during a historically bad recession.

Opportunities like those are clearly enormous for companies, but not everyone works for a company that will seize the opportunities. Yet these people can also take advantage of the recession to build their skills by applying the same principles individually. We find a highly instructive example of how that's done in techniques developed to help improve the effectiveness of psychotherapists—whose job is one that most of us feel we do at one time or another and that is in many ways analogous to most of the service jobs that dominate large economies.

Researchers at the Institute for the Study of Therapeutic Change structure the process in three steps that everyone can use: think, act, reflect. The best performers think in fine detail about what they're going to do before they do it. They develop clear goals, define exactly how they'll measure achievement, and form a detailed plan. For a manager in the badly suffering hotel industry, for example, the goal might be increasing a specific property's profitability by 10 percent from recent depressed levels. A measure of progress could be the number of room-nights filled at rates above 50 percent of the rack rate. The detailed plan might include specific negotiating strategies for major corporate customers. The key is the level of detail in each element. Research shows that mediocre performers have only general goals, measures, and plans, if they have any at all. Top performers are precise.

The act phase involves not just executing the plan but also close, constant monitoring of the results—that is, it's performance plus feedback. Again, detail is what separates the best from the rest. As the researchers say, "The sheer volume of detail gathered in assessing their performance distinguishes the exceptional from their more average counterparts."

In the final phase, reflection, the best performers review everything they've done, assess what worked and what didn't, and form a detailed new plan. In trying to understand what went wrong— something always goes wrong—average performers blame forces outside their control. Our hotel manager might blame the weather, airfares, or the unemployment rate. Great performers, by contrast, focus relentlessly on their own actions and how to alter them for better results. An excellent hotel manager who doesn't reach his goal might decide that instead of his previous tactic of offering corporate customers enhanced service just for them, he might instead offer slightly lower rates in return for a guaranteed number of room-nights per month. The great performer focuses always, and in detail, on what he can control, not on what he can't.

These examples only suggest what is possible. Anyone can grow significantly better at virtually anything by observing the principles of great performance. This recession, by pushing everyone past the limits of his or her current abilities, places us all on the first step of the process. Whether we take the next steps is for each of us to decide.

Building the Culture

When Gordon Bethune became chief of Continental Airlines in 1994, he confronted the most toxic corporate culture I've ever heard of. The previous CEO would not accept a soft drink from one of his own employees on one of his own planes if the can had been opened. On the executive floor at headquarters, armed guards flanked the locked doors leading from the elevator lobby to the offices. Inside, buttons placed at intervals along walls could be hit to call security. The situation was this: the company's leaders were afraid that the employees might try to kill them.

Continental was within days of failing when Bethune got the job—it had been through bankruptcy twice already—and Bethune realized the employees had no reason to trust him. He was the company's tenth CEO in ten years. So he got rid of the guards at headquarters, unlocked the doors, and made the employees a simple promise. Each month that Continental ranked in the top three airlines for on-time performance, everybody would get a specified bonus. The employees wouldn't have to trust him for longer than a month. As things worked out, they did their part, he paid the bonuses, and Continental was on its way to becoming highly successful and earning a spot on *Fortune*'s annual list of America's one hundred best companies to work for—a possibility that would have seemed truly outlandish a few years earlier.

Trying to change a corporate culture in a growing company during boom times is like trying to change anything else in that environment: it's almost impossible because no one feels urgency. But just as a crisis is the optimal moment for personal growth, it is also the best time for a company's own personal growth, the improvement of its culture. Time and again, that's when it happens.

Douglas Conant became CEO of Campbell's Soup in early 2001—at the onset of a recession, with the company already in free fall, and with a culture almost as bad as Continental's had been. Conant quickly called a meeting of his top executives and asked them to fill out an anonymous survey telling what they considered the company's worst problems. Not one of them would do it. They believed Conant might have a secret method of determining which executive had given which answers. Yet out of that poisonous atmosphere Conant has developed a transformed company that now earns high levels of employee engagement. It couldn't have happened if the company hadn't been in desperate trouble.

At just the time Conant arrived at Campbell's, Cisco Systems was enduring the tech bust and losing 80 percent of its value. It had once been the world's most valuable company. Now its business was collapsing. The Cisco culture wasn't toxic; on the contrary, it had been highly admired. But it was a command-and-control culture, and CEO John Chambers decided that wouldn't work in the new world he was seeing. So he began the shift to a collaborative culture. Many people doubted he could pull it off, but he did—thanks in part to a tech recession. Cisco's revamped culture is a key reason the company is performing well during this downturn.

Changing any corporate culture takes a long time, and even a record-setting recession like this one isn't long enough to do the whole job. But culture change doesn't just happen. Leaders make it happen. And if the culture needs changing, a bad recession is the ideal moment to begin the process. Though the transformation will take time, the benefits will last even longer.

Psychologists have found that humans do not make progress at a steady, even pace. Instead, we follow a pattern of surge and recover. A severe recession is obviously not a time for us to recover. It is rather the very best time for us to surge, to push ourselves ahead and develop the new skills and abilities that will change us and stay with us forever. To miss this window would be a shame. Although it may seem decidedly odd to lament that this recession will eventually end, the fact is that its passing will mean the close of a historically huge opportunity for personal growth.

CHAPTER THIRTEEN

For Next Time

Getting ready for the expansion to come—and, yes, for the recession after that

Abandoning any part of the home mortgage bonanza would have been awfully difficult in October of 2006. The global economy was still booming. Home values in the United States had just started to weaken, but conventional wisdom held that this was merely a pause in their unstoppable upward march. Interest rates were low, borrowers were still keeping up with their payments, and banks were making a fortune writing mortgages for practically anyone who walked through the door and then selling those loans to investors. Moments like that, when making money is so easy, don't happen every day.

Yet at just that moment, Jamie Dimon, CEO of JPMorgan Chase, called William King, a company executive who was vacationing in Rwanda, and yelled into the phone, "Bill, I really want you to watch out for subprime! We need to sell a lot of our positions. I've seen it before. This stuff could go up in smoke!" So Chase bailed out of a lucrative line of business, with results that are now well known. When Citigroup crumpled and Washington Mutual collapsed, Chase didn't. Though battered, it remained standing and healthy—and when the crisis hit, and weaker banks lost deposits, Chase gained them as customers fled to safety.

We've looked at many ways to manage intelligently in this recession, yet you can't help noticing that one of the most important reasons certain companies are performing well in the downturn is that like Chase, they managed intelligently before it started. It's too late for that now, but it isn't too early to be thinking about next time. Even long recessions end and are followed by expansions, which eventually beget new recessions. The best managers never become so consumed by the present that they forget their place in the cycle. Just as Dimon was thinking of the inevitable bad times to come as the good times rolled, smart managers are planning now for what they'll do when economic growth returns.

The landscape of possibilities is broad, so it's useful to think of them in distinct categories:

Engaging the outside world. Good times are when you make the friends that you'll need in bad times. We all know that, yet behaving as if we mean it takes discipline. At a spring 2009 meeting of major company CEOs, a top Obama administration official (speaking on the condition that he not be named) told the corporate chiefs bluntly that they had done a lousy job of making friends in Washington. When the government needed businesspeople to serve on task forces, he said, companies sent functionaries. But when a company wanted to lobby legislators or administration officials on a potential tax or regulatory change that would benefit them, the CEO showed up and had plenty of time. Such behavior isn't forgotten when a company suddenly appears asking for help, the official said.

CEOs change every six years or less, on average, but most governments are staffed by people who serve for much longer. The official's advice to the CEOs: "Show up every so often to talk about something that doesn't necessarily serve your immediate interests."

Managing people. The temptations to become lax on this critical issue are almost overwhelming during a boom. Virtually every

company is hiring, so recruiting the best people is at its most difficult. Instead of fighting harder than ever to attract and keep the best,
many companies will fall into the trap of suspecting that maybe they
don't need to fight terribly hard—because nearly everyone they're
hiring seems to be performing well. In good times it's easier for
people to look like stars, so evaluations tend to become less rigorous.
Managers are fooled into believing they've assembled a truly fantastic team—all A players—when they're really just in a truly fantastic
economy. Getting rid of poor performers is never fun, and in good
times managers may persuade themselves that they don't have any,
so they can skip that odious chore. Companies may even be tempted
to cut back training and development, even though money for it is
abundant, because it seems less necessary.

Pay also gets out of whack easily in an expansion. We've looked at
the wisdom of designing incentive pay so it's spread out over multiple
years. In a boom, of course, absolutely no one likes that idea. Everyone wants to get paid right now for this year's fantastic results. Caving
in to specious arguments for such a system is highly tempting.

Every one of those sins will come back to haunt a company in a
downturn. Remaining rigorous on all aspects of people management
is one of the hardest things to do during a boom because people issues are often so difficult. But in a world where human capital is
every company's most valuable asset, it's one of the most critically
important jobs.

Adjusting strategy and business model. Just as every investing strategy works in a bull market, every business strategy may seem
brilliant during an economic boom. That's the time to ask how well
the strategy or business model would hold up in a recession. Some
models—especially low-price models like Wal-Mart's or Southwest Airlines's—work great through every part of the economic cycle.
But others don't. Selling diamonds in a luxurious retail environment
isn't an attractive business in a deep recession, and many jewelers
have failed in this downturn. (Selling diamonds cheap is another mat-

ter; Wal-Mart is America's largest jeweler.) Flying all-business-class jets across the Atlantic, as Eos and Silverjet used to do, wasn't a winning strategy for a recession—both companies failed soon after this downturn started—yet investors put millions of dollars into those businesses during the good times.

Those are the times to redesign your model so it will work even in a recession. FedEx, for example, makes sure that its jet fleet includes a number of older planes that are fully depreciated. As founder and CEO Fred Smith has told me, "We can go park them in the desert when times get bad." Built-in flexibility is valuable, but it needs to be built in long before the downturn arrives.

Staying connected with customers. The best companies never stop refining their customer value propositions—observing customer behavior, understanding how customer needs are changing, and experimenting with hypotheses for new value propositions. This is another form of discipline that's easy to lose when the money is rolling in, but its tremendous advantage is that it will always supply an early warning when the economy begins to tank. U.S. consumer spending started to shift toward low-price retailers in the summer of 2007—five months before the recession began. Companies that were on top of the trend could start preparing their responses long before official figures confirmed what was going on.

Managing capital. When a company lands in a recession after years of poor capital management, the pain is extreme. The company suddenly realizes it has way too much capital tied up in excess inventories, which it needs to get rid of—yet the downturn is the worst possible moment to be selling anything in larger-than-usual quantities, since customers are probably placing smaller-than-usual orders. The company's receivables and payables need to be shaped up, but it's the worst moment for doing that, also, because every company's payables are someone else's receivables, and everyone is trying to tighten simultaneously. Because the company hasn't been managed for value, its cost of capital is probably higher than that of competi-

tors, so it will pay a higher price than they will if it needs new capital to carry it through the downturn.

All that misery can be avoided if a company manages capital rigorously when times are good. That means avoiding all the mistakes just described, plus avoiding another giant one that many companies make during booms: paying too much for acquisitions. A high-priced deal may look sensible in an expansion, but when the inevitable recession strikes, the profits of the acquired company will probably wither—though the costs of the capital invested in it won't. That's one of the many bitter lessons from AOL's expensive acquisition of Time Warner, a deal that was announced at the apex of the dot-com bubble and that closed a year later, just two months before the 2001 recession began.

By contrast, companies that avoid dumb deals in a boom remain financially strong enough to make smart ones in a downturn. In the tech world, Cisco, Oracle, and IBM have all been active buyers in this recession. The benefits of wise capital management play out on a less exalted scale as well. When the Wickes furniture retailing chain filed for bankruptcy early in this recession, more than a hundred truckloads of furniture were on their way to its stores; a Milwaukee retailer that had remained financially solid, Steinhafels, bought the contents of several at bargain prices.

Getting more efficient and productive. Good times are called fat years for a reason. They're when companies as well as people get fat. And in companies, just as in people, the process is almost imperceptible until suddenly it's a big problem. The CEO of one of America's largest grocers told me that when the company went looking for efficiencies in this recession, it discovered that it was selling fifteen different sizes of rotisserie chickens, most of which differed from one another by only an ounce. By standardizing on just two sizes, it's saving $15 million a year. The company also discovered that its deli departments were using more than a hundred different types of spoons. It settled on just two—one with slots, one without. "The

customers didn't care," the CEO said. Those senseless inefficiencies and many more built up slowly over years and weren't even noticed until the company went on a diet.

The trouble is that diets don't work, for people or for companies. The only answer is a different way of life, and that's hard to introduce when times are good. Nonetheless, it must be done. What sometimes helps is introducing a new way of measuring performance, and for many companies that's a good idea in any case. As we've seen, no company can hope to be optimally efficient and productive until it understands the economic profitability of its operations at every level. Adopting such a form of measurement is guaranteed to get everyone's attention, and pushing for continual improvements can become a strong foundation for the company's new, slimmer way of life.

Adapting to changing risks. For unsuccessful companies, risk is a hot topic at the depths of a recession. For great companies, it's a hot topic at the height of a boom. It's another element of the discipline of thinking about very bad possibilities when everything seems to be perfect. Managers who do that may appear strange or foolish; Jamie Dimon certainly looked out of step when he took Chase out of subprime mortgages. The payoff from forcing managers to stretch their minds, to imagine and talk about seemingly impossible risks, is obvious only when it's too late.

Listening to unpopular thinkers always helps. We saw earlier how the views of some on what we might call the responsible fringe turned out to be on the money. At least as important is listening to one's own inner voice. It's always there, and most of us muffle it too readily. I've been struck by the number of people who told me, once the recession was under way, that in the good times they were saying to themselves, "This is crazy—it can't last!" They all remember thinking it, but I don't remember their saying it to me back when the economy was booming. And most didn't take action back then as if they believed it.

Continuing to grow personally. All the dangers that good times hold for the results of a business have their analog in dangers to the nature of a person and of a corporate culture. When everything is going well, it seems obvious to each of us that we are an overall terrific human being. The effect can be even more extreme in organizations. During the months before Enron's collapse, the firm's top executives were telling employees enthusiastically that Enron was well on its way to becoming "the world's greatest company." That's the type of hubris that the world's genuinely great companies and great people never permit themselves to go near—especially when times are at their best.

Doing all those things during an economic expansion is hard, the temptations to avoid them being considerable. Making headway on them will strengthen any company enormously. At the same time, even if a company manages to do all of them, the lessons of the Tour de France remind us that gaining ground against competitors is not easy when the road is flat and smooth. Managing intelligently during the next expansion, vital as it is, will be less a chance to clobber competitors than a way of preparing the organization for the make-or-break environment of the next recession.

That way of thinking may seem strange. It feels backward. Good times seen merely as preparation for the bad? But it is the inescapable result of thinking about your company as an institution that with luck will last longer than your career or anyone else's, persisting through the elation and challenges of economic cycles that will never end.

Keeping those cycles in mind is harder than it used to be because they're less frequent. From the Great Depression until the early 1960s, recessions arrived every four years or so. Managers didn't think about them so much as feel them. Because several could be expected in the course of a person's career, they became part of the rhythm of work. But over the past twenty-seven years we've had only four recessions, counting this one, and the two previous ones were so mild that they barely qualified for the term. We've forgotten how to think about business as progressing through a series of cycles.

Yet that's what it is and will always be. Now that we've been powerfully reminded of that fact, we can again appreciate a larger truth about life in business. Good times are when you'll experience your greatest success. But bad times—these times, the Alps—are your greatest opportunity.

Index